MATH ADVENTURES

A Key to Academic Math Advancement

GRADE 2

_____

_____

_____

Author: Ace Academic Publishing

Ace Academic Publishing is a leading supplemental educational workbook publisher for grades K-12. At Ace Academic Publishing, we realize the importance of imparting analytical and critical thinking skills during the early ages of childhood and hence our books include materials that require multiple levels of analysis and encourage the students to think outside the box.

The materials for our books are written by award winning teachers with several years of teaching experience. All our books are aligned with the state standards and are widely used by many schools throughout the country.

Prepaze is a sister company of Ace Academic Publishing. Intrigued by the unending possibilities of the internet and its role in education, Prepaze was created to spread the knowledge and learning across all corners of the world through an online platform. We equip ourselves with state-of-the-art technologies so that knowledge reaches the students through the quickest and the most effective channels.

For inquiries and bulk orders, contact Ace Academic Publishing at the following address:
Ace Academic Publishing
3031 Village Market Place,
Morrisville, NC 27560, USA
www.aceacademicpublishing.com

ISBN: 978-1-962517-09-6

Introduction

About the Book

Welcome to "**Math Adventures - A Key to Academic Math Advancement**"! This workbook is specifically designed to align with the school curriculum and help students improve their analytical and logical thinking skills. With over **750 questions and several word problems**, this book aims to cover all the required syllabus for students in Grade 2.

Our workbook is an excellent resource for end-of-the-year state tests given by schools, as well as a great review book during the summer. Whether you are looking to improve your math skills or simply keep them sharp, "**Math Adventures**" provides a comprehensive and challenging set of problems to help you achieve your goals.

Our authors have extensive experience in teaching and developing math curricula for students at all levels. **They have carefully crafted each problem to challenge students and help them develop key problem-solving and critical thinking skills.** The book covers a wide range of topics, including arithmetic, algebra, geometry, and data analysis, providing students with a well-rounded education in math.

We believe that with practice, anyone can master math. "**Math Adventures**" is designed to help students build confidence in their abilities and develop a love for the subject. With clear explanations, helpful hints, and detailed solutions, this book is an excellent tool for anyone looking to improve their math skills.

Thank you for choosing "**Math Adventures - A Key to Academic Math Advancement**". We hope that you find it useful and enjoyable!

Common Core Math Workbooks

Common Core English Workbooks

The One Big Book Workbooks

Math Adventures Workbooks

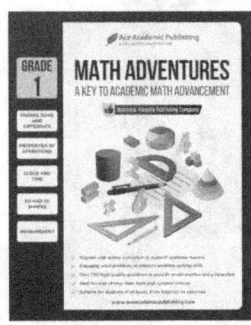 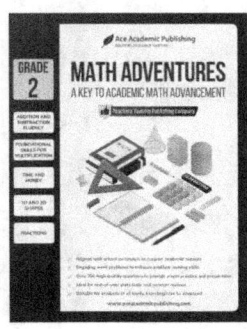  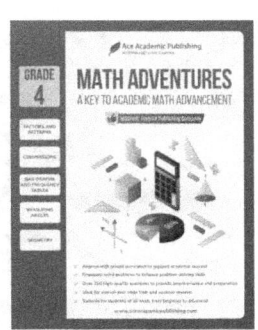

 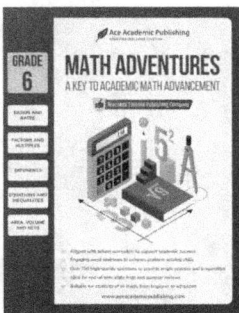  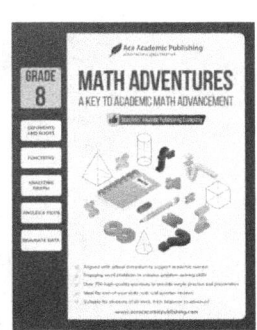

Early Learning Workbooks

TABLE OF CONTENTS

TABLE OF CONTENTS

CHAPTER 1

ADDITION AND SUBTRACTION

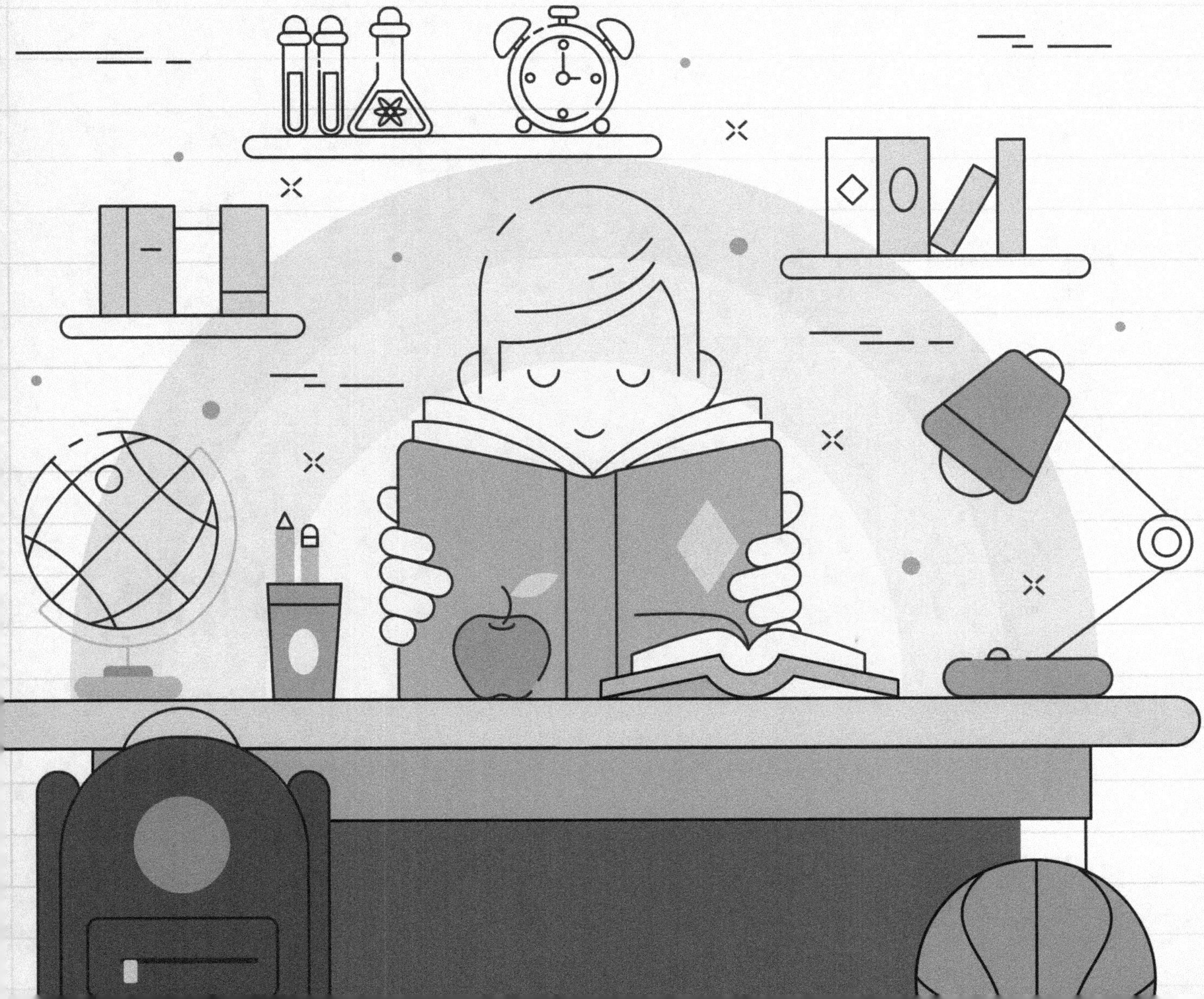

ADDITION AND SUBTRACTION FLUENCY

<u>Addition</u> is a strategy you can use to help easily solve simple addition problems.

Original Number → **3 + 5 = 8** ← Final Answer/ Number

↑
Amount you count up

You start with the original number (the first number in the equation), which in this problem is 3. Then, you count up from that number with whatever the second number in the equation is. In this equation the second number is 5, so you have to count up 5 from 3 (4, 5, 6, 7, 8). You can do this counting in your head. You can also use your fingers to help you count up.

<u>Subtraction</u> is a strategy you can use to help easily solve simple subtraction problems.

Original Number → **9 – 3 = 6** ← Final Answer/ Number

↑
Amount you count down

You start with the original number (the first number in the equation), which in this problem is 9. Then, you count down from that number with whatever the second number in the equation is. In this equation the second number is 3, so you have to count down 3 from 9 (8, 7, 6). You can do this counting in your head. You can also use your fingers to help you count.

ADDITION AND SUBTRACTION

1.1   Addition and Subtraction Fluency

Use the counting up and counting down strategies

1 Shiny has 5 apples, then she gets 6 more apples. How many apples does she have now?

(A) 11   (B) 15   (C) 10   (D) 12

2 Madison has 10 toy cars. Then, she buys 7 more cars. How many cars does she have now?

(A) 14   (B) 21   (C) 17   (D) 80

3 There are 50 students in the museum. 7 students leave the museum for lunch. How many students are still in the museum?

(A) 47   (B) 43   (C) 57   (D) 42

4 Alen is 23 years old. Cady is 5 years younger (less) than Alen. How old is Cady?

(A) 18   (B) 27   (C) 17   (D) 19

5 Benny is 31 years old. Brigette is 3 years older (more) than Benny. How old is Brigette?

(A) 33   (B) 34
(C) 37   (D) 39

Addition and Subtraction Fluency 1.1

6 Robert is thinking of a number that is less than 20, the sum of 6 and 10. What number is he thinking of?

(A) 15   (B) 16   (C) 4   (D) 11

7 Ms. Frederick brought 31 sandwiches for lunch. 8 of them were taken by her friends and the rest were packed for a picnic. How many sandwiches were packed?

(A) 21   (B) 23   (C) 39   (D) 27

8 Jim had 19 boxes. He lost one box while moving but then he received 4 new boxes from a nearby shop. How many boxes does Jim have now?

(A) 22   (B) 27   (C) 17   (D) 25

9 Jeana had 5 roses. She picked 21 lily flowers from her garden. Sushi gave 13 yellow flowers to Jeana. How many flowers does Jeana have now?

(A) 30   (B) 39   (C) 33   (D) 26

ADDITION AND SUBTRACTION

1.1   Addition and Subtraction Fluency

10 In a box, there are 25 red and black balls. The box has 7 red balls.
How many black balls are there in the box?

(A) 15   (B) 32   (C) 18   (D) 13

11 Joe has 12 ribbons. Mia gave Joe 13 more ribbons.
How many ribbons does Joe have?

(A) 31   (B) 23   (C) 22   (D) 25

12 Pizza Hut sold 63 pizzas today. They still
have 57 pizzas left to sell. How many
pizzas did they start with?

(A) 120   (B) 110

(C) 150   (D) 115

13 Mary had 27 peaches and gave 12 peaches to her friend.
She gave 6 to her mother. Shelly gave 3 peaches to Mary.
How many peaches does Mary have now?

(A) 12   (B) 17   (C) 22   (D) 11

14 Use the counting up and counting down strategies
$89 + 10 - 25 = $ _____.

Addition and Subtraction Fluency   1.1

15 During lunch, they sold 15 sandwiches and 23 juice boxes. For dinner, they sold 18 sandwiches and 27 juice boxes. How many sandwiches were sold in total?

(A) 39   (B) 27   (C) 33   (D) 28

16 There are 87 Monkeys in a zoo. 9 Monkeys were sold. How many monkeys were left in the zoo?

(A) 97   (B) 78   (C) 72   (D) 63

17 Mini had 2 cups and then received 9 from Nancy. She had to give 5 it to her neighbor. How many cups does the Mini have remaining?

(A) 7   (B) 6   (C) 11   (D) 13

18 Use the counting up and counting down strategies.
13 − 0 + 11 = _____.

(A) 23   (B) 2   (C) 1   (D) 24

1.1   **Addition and Subtraction Fluency**

19   Rina drew 10 pictures on Monday. On Tuesday, she drew 3 more pictures. How many pictures did she draw on both days?

(A) 17   (B) 11   (C) 13   (D) 15

20   Andrew had 10 bananas. He fed 2 bananas to a monkey. How many bananas does Andrew have?

(A) 5   (B) 7

(C) 8   (D) 11

Next Section: Addition of Two and Three-Digit Numbers ❯❯

ADDITION OF TWO AND THREE-DIGIT NUMBERS

In the method of Adding two digits, you can add 2 two-digit numbers together.

To add together 24 and 13 line the numbers up vertically, so the numbers in the ones place (4 and 3) line up and the numbers in the tens place (2 and 1) line up. You start by adding in the ones place, so you add together 4 and 3. That equals 7, so you write the number 7 below the two numbers you are adding together in the ones place. Then, you add together the numbers in the tens place. You add together 2 and 1, which equals 3. Write this number 3 below the two numbers you are adding together in the tens place. The answer to the addition equation is 37.

$$
\begin{array}{r}
2\ 4 \\
+\ 1\ 3 \\
\hline
3\ 7
\end{array}
$$

↑   ↑
Tens Ones

You can add 3 digit numbers together.

To add together 372 and 615 line the numbers up vertically, so the numbers in the ones place (2 and 5), the tens place (7 and 1), and the hundreds place (3 and 6) all line up. Start by adding in the ones place, so add together 2 and 5. That equals 7, so write the number 7 below the two numbers you are adding together in the ones place. Then, add in the tens place, so add together 7 and 1.

$$
\begin{array}{r}
3\ 7\ 2 \\
6\ 1\ 5 \\
\hline
9\ 8\ 7
\end{array}
$$

↑ ↑ ↑
Hundreds Tens Ones

That equals 8, so write the number 8 below the numbers you are adding together in the tens place. Finally, add in the hundreds place, so add together 3 and 6. That equals 9, so write the number 9 below the numbers you are adding together in the hundreds place.

ADDITION AND SUBTRACTION

1.2   **Addition of Two and Three-Digit Numbers**

Add together the two and three-digit numbers to solve the word problems.

1 Lynton has 17 black balls and 21 white balls. How many balls does Lynton have in total?

(A) 47   (B) 38   (C) 27   (D) 35

2 Madlyn has 27 apples. Chris has 10 apples. How many apples do they have together?

(A) 47   (B) 38   (C) 37   (D) 35

3 Add together 3 and 4 two-digit numbers.
57 + 21 + 10 + 33 = _____.

(A) 111   (B) 121   (C) 107   (D) 125

4 There are 15 monkeys, 23 elephants, 9 lions, and 47 deer in the zoo. How many animals are in the zoo?

(A) 100   (B) 120   (C) 94   (D) 114

5 The shop has 57 onion baskets and 62 potato baskets. How many total baskets are there?

(A) 119   (B) 200   (C) 229   (D) 105

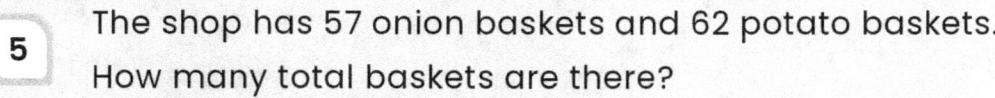

Addition of Two and Three-Digit Numbers   1.2

Add the two and three-digit numbers to solve the word problems.

6 Rachel has 129 pies. She sells 20 pies at her restaurant. How many pies does she have left?

A) 159   B) 199   C) 189   D) 149

7 There are 107 children playing in the park. 25 children come later to the park. How many children are all together in the park?

A) 139   B) 132   C) 125   D) 177

8 Teddy has 119 coins and Marlin received 231 coins from her mom. How many coins have they collected in all?

A) 350   B) 290   C) 410   D) 320

9 Add these three-digit numbers. 541 + 374 = _____.

A) 915   B) 834   C) 742   D) 952

10 Add these three-digit numbers. 222 + 624 = _____.

A) 956   B) 756   C) 846   D) 806

ADDITION AND SUBTRACTION

1.2   Addition of Two and Three-Digit Numbers

Add three-digit numbers to solve the word problem.

11   Jim has 455 chicks. He buys 551 more chicks. How many chicks does Jim have now?

(A) 1001   (B) 1011

(C) 1006   (D) 1150

12   Calvin and Edwin were playing cards. Calvin had 27 cards with him and Edwin had 25 cards. How many cards were there in total?

(A) 52   (B) 59   (C) 53   (D) 56

13   Kenny has 223 milk chocolates, Teddy has 115 dark chocolates and Simon has 133 wafer chocolates. How many chocolates do they have altogether?

(A) 411   (B) 570   (C) 500   (D) 471

14   Henry has 4 tickets to a show. Two of the tickets cost 125 pounds each, and the other two tickets cost 150 pounds. How much is the total cost of the tickets in British pounds?

(A) 750   (B) 680   (C) 550   (D) 590

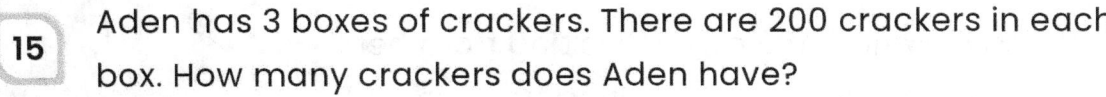 **Addition of Two and Three-Digit Numbers** | **1.2**

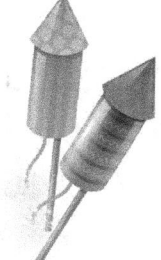

15 Aden has 3 boxes of crackers. There are 200 crackers in each box. How many crackers does Aden have?

(A) 700   (B) 500   (C) 600   (D) 900

16 In an aquarium, there are 53 catfish and 21 dolphins. How many fish are there altogether?

(A) 94   (B) 74   (C) 60   (D) 85

17 Augustin has 215 stamps. He collects 55 stamps from his mother and 102 from his cousins. How many stamps does Augustin have?

(A) 372   (B) 330   (C) 300   (D) 375

18 Andres, Mike, Joe, and Mary all have 160 books each. How many books do they have altogether?

(A) 600   (B) 650   (C) 640   (D) 740

1.2   **Addition of Two and Three-Digit Numbers**

19 At a party, Lavinia had 450 guests visiting from her side, and Carol had 290 guests visiting from her side. Also, 350 kids were planning to attend the party. How many total guests attended the party?

(A) 950   (B) 1090   (C) 1119   (D) 1500

20 Add these two and three-digit numbers.

35 + 353 = _____.

(A) 333   (B) 382   (C) 388   (D) 392

Next Section: Subtraction of Two and Three-Digit Numbers

SUBTRACTION OF TWO AND THREE-DIGIT NUMBERS

In the Subtracting two digits method you group ones into a group of ten, or tens into a group of one hundred to help you solve an addition or subtraction problem.

Sometimes you need to use regrouping to help solve subtraction problems with two-digit numbers.

$$
\begin{array}{r}
9\ 1 \\
-\ 4\ 6 \\
\hline
?\ ? \\
\end{array}
$$

The first number is 91. The second number is 46. You start subtracting in the ones place. You cannot take 6 ones away from 1 one. In order to have enough ones you can take 1 of the groups of ten and regroup it into 10 ones.

If you add the original 1 one that was in the ones place and the 10 ones you regrouped from the tens place (1 + 10), there are now 11 ones in the top of the ones place.

$$
\begin{array}{r}
^{8}\quad{}^{11} \\
9\ \ \cancel{1} \\
-\ 4\ 6 \\
\hline
?\ 5 \\
\end{array}
$$

$$
\begin{array}{r}
^{8}\quad{}^{11} \\
9\ \ \cancel{1} \\
-\ 4\ 6 \\
\hline
4\ 5 \\
\end{array}
$$

If you take 6 ones away from 11 ones, there are 5 ones left. Write this as the answer in the ones place. Now subtract in the tens place.

There are now 8 tens in the top of the tens place because one of the groups of ten was regrouped into ones. If you take 4 tens away from 8 tens, there are 4 tens left. Write this as the answer in the tens place. The final answer is 45.

SUBTRACTION OF TWO AND THREE-DIGIT NUMBERS

Sometimes you need to use regrouping to help solve subtraction problems with three digit numbers.

```
  6 8 3
- 2 2 7
  ? ? ?
```

The first number is 683. The second number is 227. You start subtracting in the ones place. You cannot take 7 ones away from 3 ones. In order to have enough ones you can take 1 of the groups of ten and regroup it into 10 ones.

If you add the original 3 ones that was in the ones place and the 10 ones you regrouped from the tens place (3 + 10), there are now 13 ones in the top of the ones place.

```
      7  13
  6   8   3
- 2   2   7
  ?   ?   ?
```

```
      7  13
  6   8   3
- 2   2   7
  ?   ?   6
```

If you take 7 ones away from 13 ones, there are 6 ones left. Write this as the answer in the ones place. Now subtract in the tens place.

There are now 7 tens in the top of the tens place because one of the groups of ten was regrouped into ones. If you take 2 tens away from 7 tens, there are 5 tens left. Write this as the answer in the tens place.

```
      7  13
  6   8   3
- 2   2   7
  ?   5   6
```

```
  6 8 3
- 2 2 7
  ? 5 6
```

Now subtract in the hundreds place

If you take 2 hundreds away from 6 hundreds, there are 4 hundreds left. Write this as the answer in the hundreds place. The final answer is 456.

```
  6 8 3
- 2 2 7
  4 5 6
```

Subtraction of Two and Three-Digit Numbers   **1.3**

> Use regrouping to solve the subtraction equations and the word problem.

1 Use regrouping to solve the subtraction equation.
914 - 523 = _____.

(A) 391   (B) 415   (C) 355   (D) 425

2 Andrew and Frederick had 836 blackboards. They gave 515 blackboards to an orphanage. How many blackboards were remaining?

(A) 391   (B) 321   (C) 415   (D) 236

3 There are 83 students in a class. Out of that 19 are from Hostel. How many students come from Home?

(A) 72   (B) 69   (C) 64   (D) 75

4 In a supermarket, there are 965 boxes to be delivered. On Monday, they delivered 113 boxes, and on Tuesday, they delivered 335 boxes. How many boxes still have to be delivered?

(A) 417   (B) 570   (C) 655   (D) 517

5 Bob bought 37 candies. Out of these, he gave 9 candies to his sister. How many candies are now left with Bob?

(A) 30   (B) 28   (C) 25   (D) 31

1.3   **Subtraction of Two and Three-Digit Numbers**

6 Cathy's mom is 45 years old. Cathy and her mom's age difference is 23. Calculate Cathy's age?

(A) 22   (B) 15   (C) 25   (D) 17

7 Rio has 121 garlands with him. Edison has 43 fewer garlands than Rio. How many garlands does Edison have?

(A) 87   (B) 75   (C) 92   (D) 78

8 Alisa spends 70 dollars on groceries. She spends 25 dollars on vegetables. Calculate how much she spent on other groceries.

(A) 75   (B) 65   (C) 45   (D) 55

9 There were 107 parrots in a cage. Shiny gave 16 parrots to her friend. How many parrots were still in the cage?

(A) 85   (B) 73   (C) 81   (D) 91

10 Vinci has 413 batches. Allen has more batches than Vinci. Together they have 900 batches. How many batches does Allen have?

(A) 450   (B) 487   (C) 585   (D) 617

Subtraction of Two and Three-Digit Numbers | 1.3

11 There are 881 packages in a factory. They sell 425 packages. How many packages are remaining in the factory?

(A) 452   (B) 478   (C) 456   (D) 425

12 In a box, there are 850 apples. 333 apples are labeled. How many apples are unlabeled in the box?

(A) 533   (B) 450   (C) 673   (D) 517

Use regrouping to solve the subtraction equations and to solve the two step word problems.

---

13 Rapunzel has 5 boxes of spaghetti. There are 108 spaghetti in each box. How much spaghetti does Rapunzel have? She cooks and eats 93 spaghetti. How much spaghetti does she have left?

_____

14 Lisa and Adam have 187 flowers. They give 22 of them to their family. How many flowers do they have left? They give 93 of them to their friends. How many flowers does Lisa and Adam have left?

_____

ADDITION AND SUBTRACTION

15 There are 232 women in a stadium. If there are a total of 450 people at the stadium, how many men are there?

(A) 232   (B) 252   (C) 218   (D) 273

Use regrouping to solve the subtraction equations and the word problem.

---

16 Sherlyn has 567 bottles. Linda has 331 bottles. How many more bottles does Sherlyn have than Linda?

(A) 200   (B) 236   (C) 323   (D) 150

17 Judith weighs 81 lbs. and Mabel is 21 lbs less than Judith. Calculate Mabel's weight?

(A) 80   (B) 56   (C) 60   (D) 51

18 There are 57 dishes to clean. Jason cleaned 16 dishes. How many dishes are left to clean?

(A) 45   (B) 30

(C) 41   (D) 49

Subtraction of Two and Three-Digit Numbers | **1.3**

19 Mercy had 133 earrings to be sold in a month. At the end of the month, she had 77 earrings remaining. How many did Mercy sell?

(A) 60   (B) 89   (C) 56   (D) 46

20 In a group of 770 people, 555 people loved coffee, and the other group loved tea. How many people loved tea?

(A) 230   (C) 315   (B) 333   (D) 215

Next Section: Word Problems Involving Addition and Subtraction ≫

WORD PROBLEMS INVOLVING ADDITION AND SUBTRACTION

A word problem of addition and subtraction written as one sentence to apply a **'real-life'** scenario and also using keywords for addition or subtraction (plus, more, minus, difference.,)

Example:

Mr. Noah brought 20 burgers for dinner. 10 of them were taken by his friends and the rest were packed for a picnic. How many burgers are packed?

Number of burgers = 20

Rest of burgers = 20 - 10 = 10.

Word Problems Involving Addition and Subtraction

1.4

1 Amelia has 23 Balls. 7 of them are small rubber balls and the rest are smiley balls. How many smiley balls does Amelia have?

(A) 15   (B) 16   (C) 12   (D) 9

2 Kristen had 57 mangoes. She bought 15 more mangoes from market. How many mangoes does she have now?

(A) 70   (B) 80   (C) 72   (D) 67

3 There is a box of 100 ice cream bars. The box has 44 chocolate ice cream bars, and the remaining bars are vanilla. How many vanilla ice cream bars are available in the box?

(A) 55   (B) 69   (C) 56   (D) 73

4 A garden has 103 rose plants, 99 lemon plants, 50 lily plants and 176 crotons. How many total plants are found in the garden?

(A) 370   (B) 457   (C) 428   (D) 393

1.4

Word Problems Involving Addition and Subtraction

5 John's sandwich shop has sold 53 sandwiches today. They still have 79 sandwiches to sell. How many sandwiches did they start with?

(A) 132   (B) 140   (C) 128   (D) 135

6 Judith has 5 boxes. The first 3 boxes have 11 Choco sticks in each box. The last 2 boxes have 25 Choco sticks each. Calculate how many Choco sticks Judith has in total.

(A) 100   (B) 83   (C) 89   (D) 91

7 In a theater, there were 500 seats. 112 of the seats were occupied by staff members and 203 were occupied by children. How many seats were available for the parents?

(A) 200   (B) 173   (C) 185   (D) 191

8 Becky's grandmother gave her 135 rubber bands. Her dad gave her 93 more. Becky gave 13 rubber bands each to her two brothers. How many rubber bands are left with Becky?

(A) 182   (B) 202   (C) 197   (D) 185

Word Problems Involving Addition and Subtraction

1.4

9 On a school bus, there were 37 children going to school. At a stop, some more children got on the bus. Then there were 66 children altogether in the bus. How many children got on the bus at the bus stop?

Ⓐ 32 Ⓑ 29 Ⓒ 15 Ⓓ 25

10 Haden has taken 31 books from the library. He just finished reading 13 of the books. How many books does he have left to read?

Ⓐ 18 Ⓑ 21 Ⓒ 15 Ⓓ 23

Use the make-an-equation strategy to solve the addition and subtraction word problems.

11 Sierra walks 1047 meters in a week. She walks 315 fewer meters the next week. How many meters did Sierra walk?

Ⓐ 650 Ⓑ 732 Ⓒ 682 Ⓓ 850

1.4 **Word Problems Involving Addition and Subtraction**

12 A group of 4 friends contributes gifts to an orphanage. The first friend gives 67 gift boxes, the second friend gives 43 gift boxes, the third friend gives 75 gift boxes, and the fourth friend gives 36 gift boxes. How many gifts did they give all together?

(A) 290

(B) 221

(C) 350

(D) 187

Use the make an equation and then draw a picture strategy to solve the two-step word problems with addition and subtraction.

13 Mercy has 5 boxes of cold drinks. Each box has 36 bottles.

a. How many bottles are there in total in the box?

   Also, Mercy sells 63 bottles

b. How many bottles does Mercy have left?

_____

14 Tyron has 89 cars in his garage. He repairs 25 cars and delivers them this week.

a. How many cars are still left in his garage?

   He receives 57 more cars to be repaired in the next week

b. How many cars does he still need to repair?

_____

15 Berlin and Benny buy 5 dresses for their family.
The rate is 89, 152, 368, 150, 297 dollars.

   a. How much is the total bill?

   Benny adds another dress which is 98 dollars

   b. How much is the total bill?

_____

16 Allen buys 6000 straws for his shop and sells 2336 straws online.
How many straws does Allen have remaining?

A) 3664   B) 4256   C) 4152   D) 3985

17 Aaron has 7665 oranges and buys 3154 oranges more from a shopkeeper. How many oranges does Aaron have in total?

A) 9845   B) 10,819

C) 10,560   D) 9600

18 The lion walks 5687 yards in a day. The tiger walks 4285 yards in a day. What is the difference in the distance the two animals walk?

A) 1402   B) 1500   C) 900   D) 1150

1.4 Word Problems Involving Addition and Subtraction

19 Bruce's age is 63 years. Cady is 23 years younger than Bruce. Linda is 7 years older than Cady. What is Linda's age?

Ⓐ 33   Ⓑ 47   Ⓒ 52   Ⓓ 42

20 Thomas bought two gold chains for 4238 dollars. The first chain cost 2336 dollars. How much did the second chain cost?

Ⓐ 2000   Ⓑ 1823   Ⓒ 1902   Ⓓ 1951

Next Section:
Addition with Regrouping

ADDITION WITH REGROUPING

Regrouping is when you group ones into a group of ten, or tens into a group of one hundred to help you solve an addition or subtraction problem.

Sometimes you need to use regrouping to help solve addition problems with two-digit numbers.

You can represent this problem with base ten blocks.

$$\begin{array}{r} 2\ \ 8 \\ +\ 1\ \ 5 \\ \hline ?\ \ ? \end{array}$$

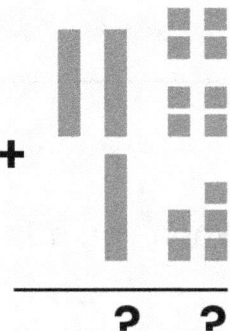

The first number is 28, which is represented in the top line by 2 tens and 8 ones. The second number is 15, which is represented in the bottom line by 1 ten and 5 ones.

You start adding in the ones place

When you add all of the ones together there are 13. There is a group of ten in this number, so you can use regrouping to help you.

ADDITION WITH REGROUPING

Ten of the ones can be regrouped into 1 ten. There are 3 ones that are left. After regrouping there is 1 ten and 3 ones.

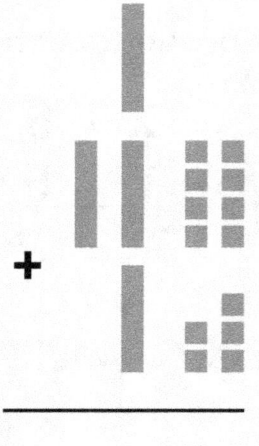

The 3 remaining ones are written as the answer in the ones place. The 1 ten that was made with regrouping is moved to the tens place.

Now add in the tens place.

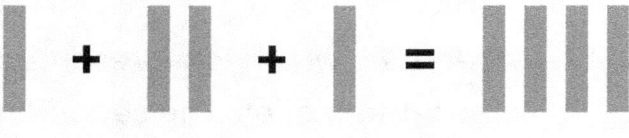

When you add together all of tens there are 4 tens.

These 4 tens are written as the answer in the tens place. In the answer there are 4 tens and 3 ones, which means the final answer is 43

$$
\begin{array}{r}
2\ \ 8 \\
+\ 1\ \ \ 5 \\
\hline
4\ \ \ 3
\end{array}
$$

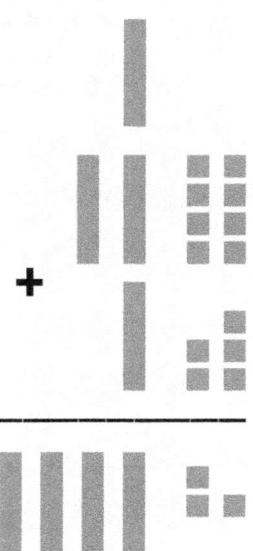

Addition with Regrouping   1.5

1 Find the answer to the addition problem represented by base ten blocks using regrouping.

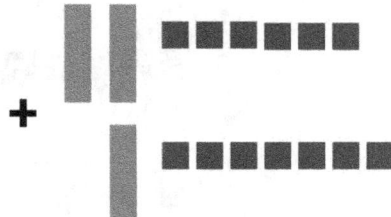

(A) 4 tens and 3 ones   (B) 5 tens and 4 ones

(C) 3 tens and 5 ones   (D) 2 tens and 6 ones

2 Find the answer to the addition problem represented by base ten blocks using regrouping.

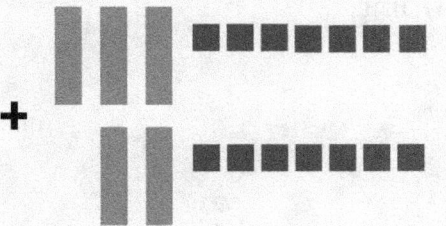

(A) 4 tens and 3 ones   (B) 6 tens and 4 ones

(C) 5 tens and 3 ones   (D) 5 tens and 4 ones

3 Find the answer to the addition problem represented by base ten blocks using regrouping.

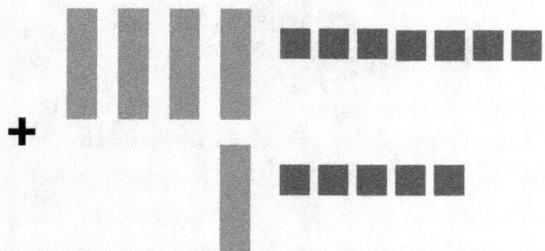

- (A) 4 tens and 3 ones
- (B) 6 tens and 4 ones
- (C) 6 tens and 2 ones
- (D) 2 tens and 6 ones

4 Find the answer to the addition problem represented by base ten blocks using regrouping.

- (A) 3 hundreds 7 tens and 8 ones
- (B) 3 hundreds 4 tens and 6 ones
- (C) 3 hundreds 2 tens and 4 ones
- (D) 2 hundreds 3 tens and 6 ones

Addition with Regrouping **1.5**

5 Find the answer to the addition problem represented by base ten blocks using regrouping.

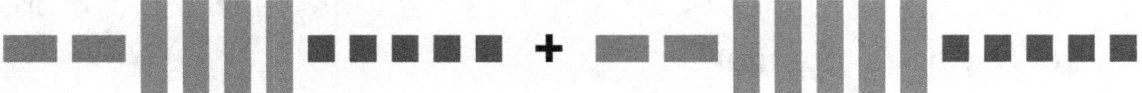

- (A) 5 hundreds 0 tens and 0 ones
- (B) 6 hundreds 3 tens and 9 ones
- (C) 5 hundreds 9 tens and 0 ones
- (D) 4 hundreds 8 tens and 5 ones

6 Find the answer to the addition problem represented by base ten blocks using regrouping.

- (A) 3 hundreds 8 tens and 9 ones
- (B) 2 hundreds 8 tens and 8 ones
- (C) 2 hundreds 9 tens and 1 ones
- (D) 4 hundreds 8 tens and 5 ones

1.5   Addition with Regrouping

Draw a picture using base ten blocks to represent the addition problem, then solve the word problem.

7   James has 49 mangoes. Mary has 34 mangoes. How many mangoes do they have together?

    (A) 83   (B) 79   (C) 75   (D) 80

8   312 + 425 = _____.

    (A) 652   (B) 720   (C) 737   (D) 746

9   Collin has 33 bags of chocolate. Robin has 26 bags of chocolate. If they put their bags of chocolate together, how many bags of chocolate will they have?

    (A) 59   (B) 65   (C) 51   (D) 63

10   Ashley buys 132 sweet corn today. The next day, she buys 323 sweet corn. How many sweet corns did Ashley buy over these two days?

    (A) 520   (B) 455   (C) 415   (D) 482

Addition with Regrouping 1.5

11 There are 3 boxes of ice cream bars in a freezer. There are 135 ice cream bars in each box. How many ice cream bars are in the freezer?

(A) 520   (B) 405   (C) 415   (D) 465

Draw a picture using base ten blocks to represent the addition problem, then solve the word problem.

---

12 Draw a picture using base ten blocks to represent the addition problem, then solve the word problem.

Is this correct? Explain why it is correct or incorrect. If it is incorrect, what could you do to correct it?

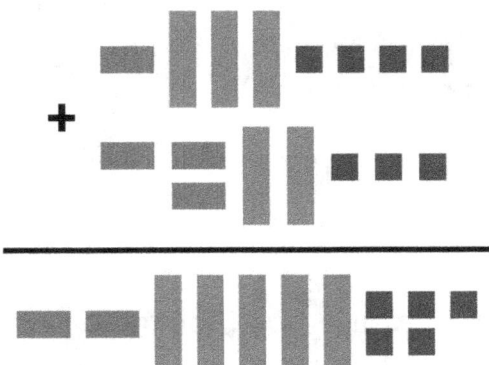

_____

13 The teacher gives the class the problem below.

Is this correct? Explain why it is correct or incorrect. If it is incorrect, what could you do to correct it?

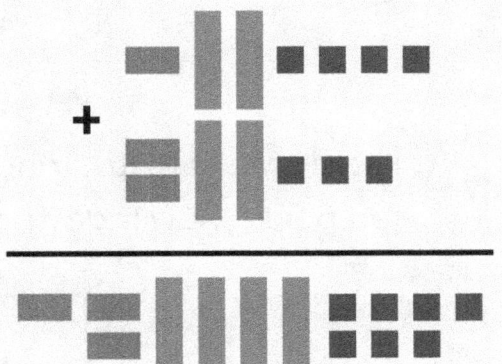

_____

1.5 **Addition with Regrouping**

14 Jerry and Melinda collect 2365 and 1025 stamps from different countries. How many stamps do they have together?

(A) 3390   (B) 4000   (C) 4325   (D) 3375

15 A dog named Andrew weighs 53 pounds and his brother weighs 40 pounds. How much do the two dogs weigh together?

(A) 85   (B) 93   (C) 95   (D) 89

16 Jane has 3 boxes of lemons. There are 1089 in each box. How many lemons does Jane have?

(A) 3233   (B) 3256   (C) 3269   (D) 3569

17 Peter owns a restaurant. He buys 2176 coffee bean packs and 1123 tea packs. How many packs did Peter buy in total?

(A) 3500   (B) 3299   (C) 3356   (D) 2996

18 There are 190 prisms shaped like cubes and 220 shaped like rectangular prisms. How many prisms are there together?

(A) 410   (B) 450   (C) 436   (D) 520

19 5269 + 4125 = _____.

(A) 9394   (B) 9865   (C) 8256   (D) 9568

20 6895 + 1156 = _____.

(A) 8000   (B) 8563   (C) 8051   (D) 8254

Next Section: Chapter Review >>

1.6 Chapter Review

Use the counting up and counting down strategies

1 Shacks has 65 figs, then she gets 20 more figs from her mom. How many figs does she have now?

(A) 90   (B) 85   (C) 82   (D) 75

2 There are 90 students in a class. 37 students leave the class for dance practice. How many students are still in the class?

(A) 47   (B) 43   (C) 53   (D) 58

3 Mary is 19 years old. Her sister Kim is double her age. How old is Kim?

(A) 29   (B) 34   (C) 38   (D) 19

4 Lucy had 55 burgers. She gave 8 burgers to her friends and bought 3 more burgers from a nearby shop. How many burgers does Lucy have now?

(A) 45   (B) 50   (C) 37   (D) 55

Add together the two and three-digit numbers to solve the word problems.

5 Cynthia has 26 yellow ribbons and 33 red ribbons. How many ribbons does Cynthia have in total?

(A) 47 (B) 49 (C) 59 (D) 55

6 There are 63 tomatoes, 55 onions, 29 potatoes, and 47 capsicum in the shop. How many vegetables are there in total?

(A) 150 (B) 194 (C) 188 (D) 165

Add and subtract three and four-digit numbers to solve the word problem.

7 Robin has 6 boxes of plates. There are 300 plates in each box. How many plates does Robin have?

(A) 1800 (B) 1500 (C) 2000 (D) 1200

8 In a marriage hall, there were 200 men, 250 women, 150 elderly people and 210 kids. How many people were there in total?

(A) 900 (B) 810 (C) 950 (D) 850

1.6   **Chapter Review**

Use regrouping to solve the subtraction equations and the word problem.

9 Matthew had 300 oranges. He sold 75 oranges. How many oranges were left over?

(A) 230   (B) 225   (C) 275   (D) 215

10 Raleigh has 360 bags with him. Jack has 127 fewer bags than Raleigh. How many bags does Jack have?

(A) 225   (B) 233   (C) 250   (D) 245

Use regrouping to solve the subtraction equation and to solve the two-step word problems.

11 Lisa has 2 boxes of toys. There are 255 toys in each box. How many toys does Lisa have? She sells 300 toys online. How many toys does she have left?

_____

12 There are 2332 girls in a school. If there are a total of 4000 children in the school, how many boys are there in the school?

(A) 2000   (B) 1732   (C) 1668   (D) 1985

13 Sherley has 107 chocolates. She bought 25 more chocolates from the market. How many chocolates does she have now?

(A) 132   (B) 140   (C) 125   (D) 123

Use the make an equation and then draw a picture strategy to solve the two-step word problems with addition and subtraction.

---

14 Mania has 4 boxes of milk powder. Each box has 60 packs.

a. How many packs are there in the box?
   Also, Mania sells 100 packs

b. How many packs does Mania have left?

_____

15 Roger buys 4300 bricks and finds 1055 bricks broken. How many unbroken bricks does Roger have?

(A) 3664   (B) 3245   (C) 3500   (D) 3852

16 Lawrence has 2565 apples and buys 3652 apples more from a shopkeeper. How many apples does Lawrence have in total?

(A) 6217   (B) 5268   (C) 6523   (D) 5217

1.6 Chapter Review

17 Find the answer to the addition problem represented by base ten blocks using regrouping.

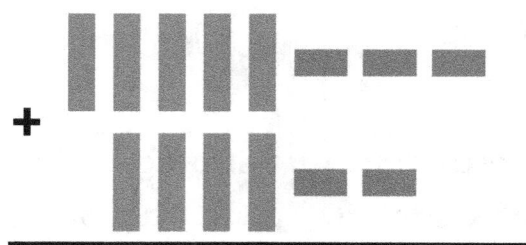

(A) 4 tens and 3 ones

(B) 9 tens and 5 ones

(C) 9 tens and 4 ones

(D) 7 tens and 5 ones

18 Alisa has 23 dollars and her friend has 54 dollars. How much do they have together?

(A) 85   (B) 93   (C) 77   (D) 73

19 At a restaurant, 135 people order noodles and 153 people order pasta. How many total orders are there?

(A) 288   (B) 350   (C) 250   (D) 285

20 $2133 + 1243 =$ _____.

(A) 3376   (B) 3500   (C) 3452   (D) 3356

Next Chapter: Foundational Skills for Multiplication

CHAPTER 2

FOUNDATIONAL SKILLS FOR MULTIPLICATION

HELP LITTLE BEAR FIND HIS FOOD

EVEN AND ODD NUMBERS

First, we have to learn what is an even number that is numbers that can be split into 2 equal groups.

Is 8 an even number or odd number? Let's check!

8 is an even number because it can be split into 2 equal groups of 4.

What is an odd number?

Numbers that cannot be split into 2 equal groups.

Is 9 an even number or odd number?

9 is an odd number because it cannot be evenly split into 2 equal groups.

2.1   **Even and Odd Numbers**

1   Identify whether 55 is an odd or an even number.

(A) Odd   (B) Even

2   Identify whether 36 is an odd or an even number.

(A) Odd   (B) Even

3   Mr. Tyke is 65 years old. Is his age an even number or an odd number?

(A) Odd   (B) Even

4   Which group has two even numbers?

(A) 48 and 50   (B) 61 and 63   (C) 51 and 52   (D) 55 and 58

5   How many apples are there in the picture? Are they odd or even number?

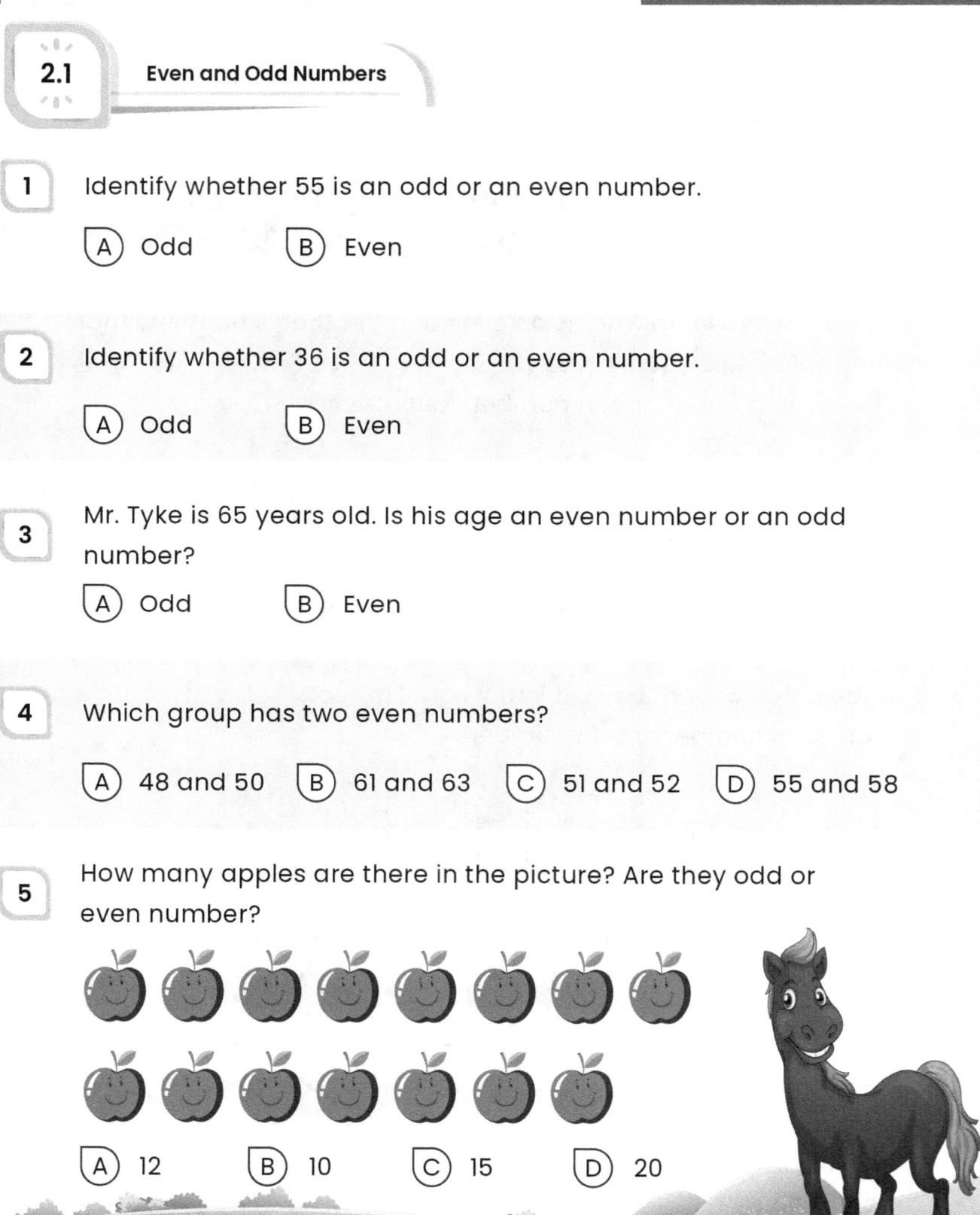

(A) 12   (B) 10   (C) 15   (D) 20

Even and Odd Numbers   **2.1**

6 James threw the dice as shown below. Find whether the sum of the two dice is even or odd?

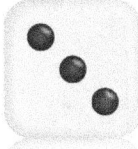  (A) Odd   (B) Even

7 How many peaches are there in the picture? Are they odd or even number?

(A) 6   (B) 10   (C) 5   (D) 8

8 Is the total sum of 75 and 13 an even or odd number?

(A) Odd   (B) Even

9 Eda had 37 cookies but she lost 8 of them while she was playing. How many cookies does she have left? Is it an odd or even number of cookies?

(A) Odd   (B) Even

10 Is the difference between 550 and 230 an even or odd number?

(A) Odd   (B) Even

2.1   **Even and Odd Numbers**

11 Sushi picked a random number of 5261. Did he pick an even or odd number?

(A) Odd   (B) Even

12 Is the total sum of 1250 and 1001 an even or odd number?

(A) Odd   (B) Even

13 There were a few students doing collage work together. Count the students below. Is there an odd or even number of students?

(A) Odd

(B) Even

14 Jane has 67 oranges and Lucy has 68 oranges. Do they have an even or odd number of oranges altogether?

(A) Odd   (B) Even

15 Is 5 more than 555 an even number or an odd number?

(A) Odd   (B) Even

Even and Odd Numbers | **2.1**

16 Write all the even numbers between 950 and 960.

_____

17 Write all the odd numbers between 1000 and 1010.

_____

18 A number is bigger than 251 and smaller than 253. Is that number an even number or an odd number? (A) Odd (B) Even

19 A number is bigger than 1290 and smaller than 1292. Is that number an even number or an odd number? (A) Odd (B) Even

20 In a volleyball game, team A scored 33 points. Team B scored 42 points. Which team scored an even number of points? (A) Team A (B) Team B

Next Section: Interpreting Arrays »

INTERPRETING ARRAYS

An array is a set of objects that are arranged in rows and columns.

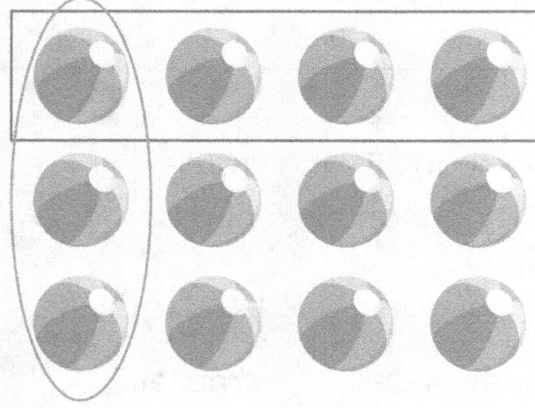

In this array, there are 3 rows and 4 columns.

This array shows 3 + 3 + 3 + 3 or 4 + 4 + 4

The total number of beach balls is 12.

1 Which array shows 3 rows and 2 columns?

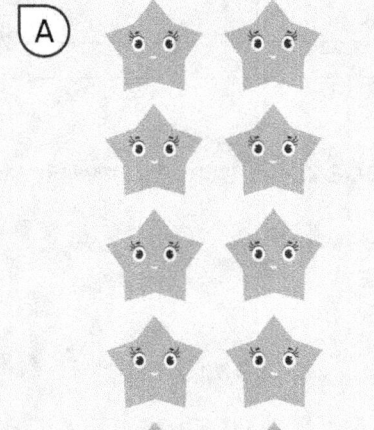

2 Which array shows 2 rows and 5 columns?

2.2   **Interpreting Arrays**

3   Which array shows 4 + 4 + 4 + 4 = ?

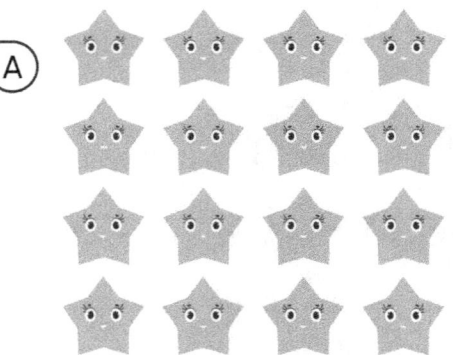

(A)

(B)

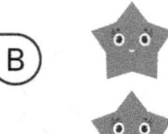

4   Madrona wants to make an array with 9 stamps. What repeated addition sentence can she make if she uses all of her stamps and makes an array?

_____

5   Sam arranges his books into 6 rows with 5 books in each row. How many books does he have? _____ books.

6   Box A has 5 rows of apples with 3 apples in each row. Box B has 6 rows of apples with 4 apples in each row. Which box has fewer apples?

(A)   Box A   (B)   Box B

Interpreting Arrays | 2.2

Look at the array below and answer the questions.

7 How many rows are there?

Ⓐ 4   Ⓑ 2

8 How many columns are there?

Ⓐ 4   Ⓑ 2

9 What is the repeated addition sentence of this array?

Ⓐ 4 + 4   Ⓑ 2 + 2

10 What is the total number of shapes?

Ⓐ 9   Ⓑ 12   Ⓒ 8   Ⓓ 10

2.2   Interpreting Arrays

> Chris, Tom, and Maddy are comparing the numbers of cakes they have.
> Look at the pictures below and answer the questions.

Chris	Tom	Maddy

11   Chris has _____ rows with _____ cakes in each row.

     (A) 3, 3   (B) 3, 2

12   What is the repeated addition sentence of Chris's array?

     (A) 4+4+4   (B) 3+3+3

13   What is the total number of Chris's cakes?

     (A) 9   (B) 12   (C) 8   (D) 10

14   Tom has _____ rows with _____ cakes in each row.

     (A) 4,3   (B) 3,4

15   What is the repeated addition sentence of Tom's array?

     (A) 4+4+4   (B) 3+3+3

16 What is the total number of Tom's cakes?

(A) 9   (B) 12   (C) 8   (D) 10

17 Maddy has _____ rows with _____ cakes in each row.

(A) 4,5   (B) 5,4

18 What is the repeated addition sentence of Maddy's array?

(A) 5+5+5+5   (B) 3+3+3+3

19 What is the total number of Maddy's cakes?

(A) 9   (B) 12   (C) 8   (D) 20

20 Who has the most cakes?

(A) Chris   (B) Tom   (B) Maddy

Next Section: Creating Arrays

63

CREATING ARRAYS

We can create an array by partitioning the rectangle into rows and columns. The small squares inside the rectangle are called units. Let's take a look at this rectangle.

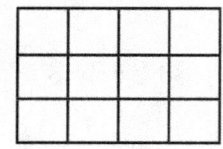

There are 3 rows and 4 columns in this rectangle.
The equation for this rectangle is 3+3+3+3 or 4+4+4
There are 12 units in this rectangle.
Now let's take a look at these rectangles.

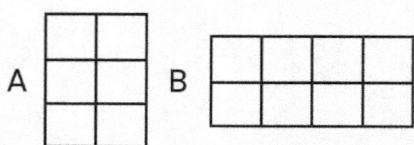

There are 3 rows, 2 columns, and 6 units in rectangle A. There are 2 rows, 4 columns, and 8 units in rectangle B.
If we add 1 row to both rectangles, which rectangle will have 8 units?

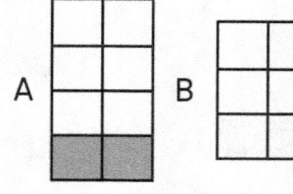

Rectangle A will have 2+2+2+2 = 8 units and rectangle B will have 4+4+4 = 12 units. So, rectangle A will have 8 units.

Creating Arrays · 2.3

1 How many rows are in this rectangle?

(A) 2 rows   (B) 4 rows

(C) 3 rows   (D) 5 rows

2 How many rows are in this rectangle?

(A) 2 rows   (B) 4 rows

(C) 3 rows   (D) 5 rows

3 How many columns are in this rectangle?

(A) 6 columns   (B) 2 columns

(C) 4 columns   (D) 5 columns

4 How many rows are in this rectangle?

(A) 6 rows   (B) 2 rows

(C) 4 rows   (D) 5 rows

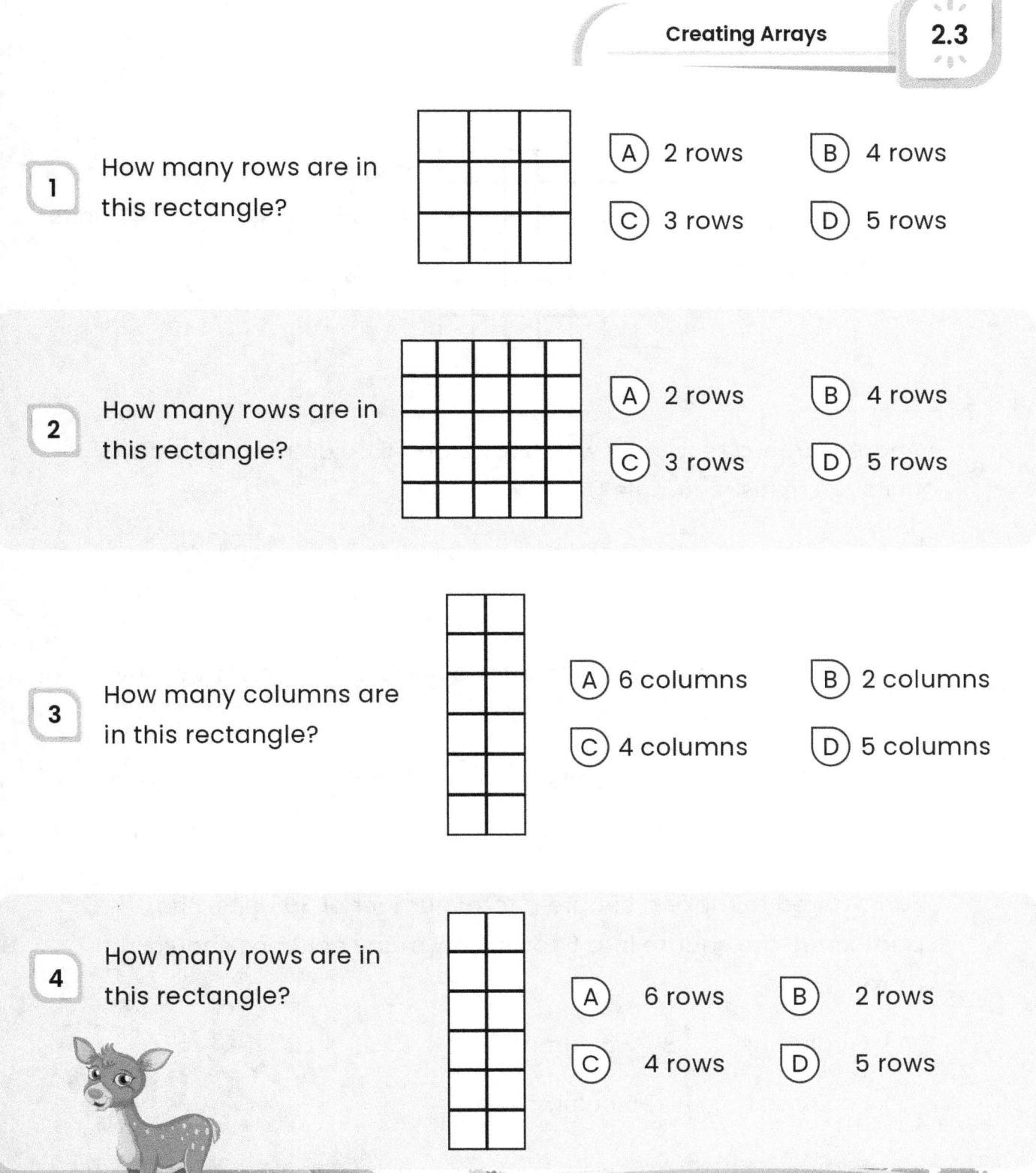

2.3   **Creating Arrays**

5 How many units are in this square?

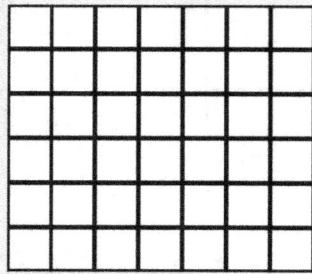

(A) 35 units   (B) 42 units

(C) 30 units   (D) 48 units

6 Andrew drew a rectangle with 5 rows and 5 columns. How many units are in his rectangle?

(A) 30 units   (B) 42 units   (C) 25 units   (D) 48 units

7 Thomas drew a rectangle with 6 rows and 2 columns. How many units are in his rectangle?

(A) 15 units   (B) 20 units   (C) 10 units   (D) 12 units

8 Eda wanted to make a square a total number of 36 units. She partitioned the square into 6 rows. How many columns should she make?

(A) 6 columns   (B) 2 columns

(C) 4 columns   (D) 5 columns

9 Beldon partitioned a rectangle into 5 columns. He wants to make 35 units. How many rows does he need to make?

(A) 6 rows　　(B) 2 rows　　(C) 4 rows　　(D) 7 rows

10 Olivia drew a rectangle with 3 rows and 4 columns. How many units are in her rectangle?

(A) 15 units　　(B) 20 units　　(C) 12 units　　(D) 10 units

11 How many columns are in this rectangle?

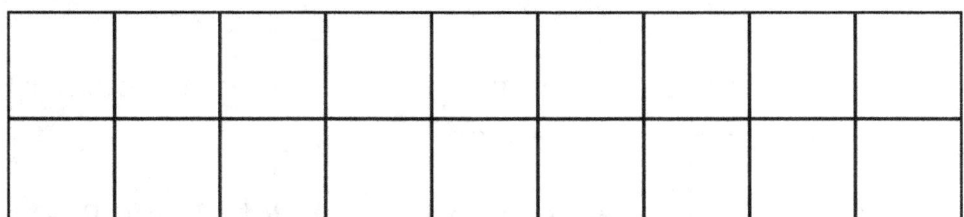

(A) 6 columns　　(B) 2 columns　　(C) 9 columns　　(D) 5 columns

2.3   **Creating Arrays**

Look at the picture and answer the questions below.

Rectangle A   Rectangle B

12 Collin wants to add rows or columns to the rectangle and make 14 units. Which rectangle can he use? Rectangle A, B, or both?

(A) Rectangle A

(B) Rectangle B

(C) Both A and B rectangles

13 Elena wants to add rows or columns to the rectangle above and make 6 units. Which rectangle can she use, Rectangle A, B, or both?

(A) Rectangle A   (B) Rectangle B   (C) Both A and B rectangles

14 Judy added 2 rows to rectangle A and 2 columns to rectangle B. Which rectangle has more units?

(A) Rectangle A   (B) Rectangle B   (C) Both A and B rectangles

15 Jack wants to add rows to the rectangle above and make 18 units. Which rectangle should he use? Rectangle A, B, or both?

(A) Rectangle A   (B) Rectangle B   (C) Both A and B rectangles

16 Allen drew a rectangle with 4 rows and 7 columns. How many units are in his rectangle?

(A) 15 units   (B) 24 units   (C) 28 units   (D) 16 units

17 Nora added 2 columns to the rectangle. How many units are in new rectangle after adding units?

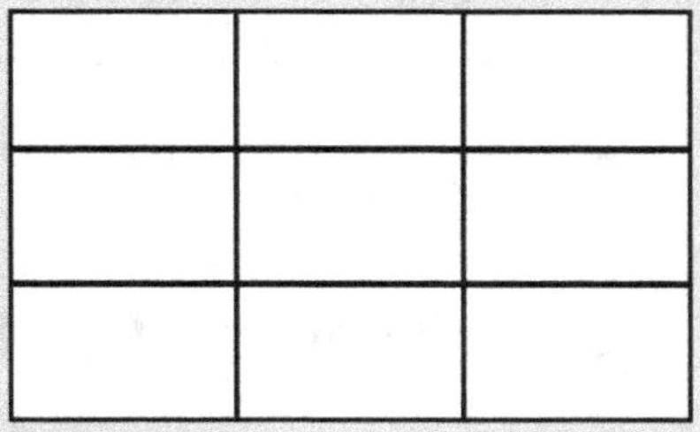

(A) 12 units   (B) 24 units

(C) 28 units   (D) 15 units

18 John partitioned a rectangle into 5 rows. How many columns does he need to make in order to make 40 units?

(A) 6 columns   (B) 2 columns   (C) 9 columns   (D) 8 columns

19 How many units are in this rectangle?

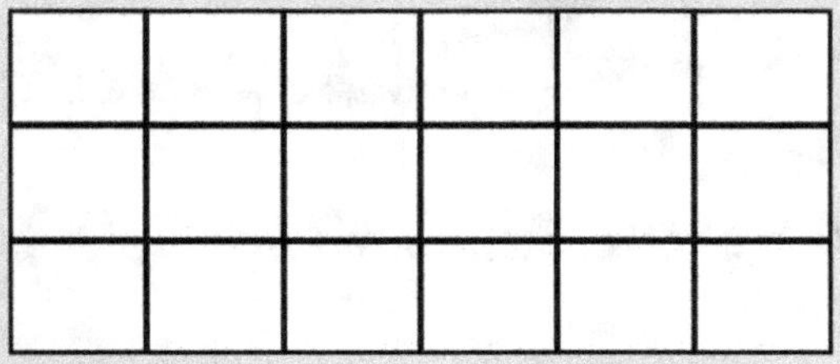

(A) 18 units   (B) 24 units

(C) 28 units   (D) 16 units

2.3   **Creating Arrays**

20   Peter added 2 rows to the rectangle below. How many units are in this rectangle after adding 2 rows?

(A) 12 units   (B) 24 units

(C) 28 units   (D) 16 units

Next Section: Chapter Review ≫

Chapter Review 2.4

1 Is 103 an odd or an even number?

(A) Odd   (B) Even

2 There are 50 students playing at the playground and 10 more students join them. Are there an even or odd number of students playing at the playground?

(A) Odd   (B) Even

3 A number is bigger than 990 and smaller than 992. Is that number an even number or odd number?

(A) Even   (B) Odd

4 Is the difference between 1550 and 1030 an even or an odd number?

(A) Odd   (B) Even

5 Is 7 more than 660 an even number or an odd number?

(A) Even   (B) Odd

6 How many peaches are there in the picture?
Is that an odd or even number?

(A) 11   (B) 8

(C) 9   (D) 6

2.4 Chapter Review

Look at the array below and answer the questions.

7 How many rows are there?

Ⓐ 3   Ⓑ 2

8 How many columns are there?

Ⓐ 2   Ⓑ 3

9 What is the repeated addition sentence of this array?

Ⓐ 3+3   Ⓑ 2−2

10 What is the total number of shapes?

Ⓐ 6   Ⓑ 9   Ⓒ 8   Ⓓ 10

11 Mary arranges her books into 3 rows with 4 books in each row. How many books does she have? _____ book.

12 Box A has 4 rows of chocolates with 4 chocolates in each row.
Box B has 4 rows of chocolates with 3 chocolates in each row.
Which box has more chocolates?

Ⓐ Box A   Ⓑ Box B

Chapter Review 2.4

13 Rocky picked a random number which is 2334. Did he pick an even or odd number?

(A) Even (B) Odd

14 Which group has two even numbers?

(A) 98 and 108 (B) 111 and 113

(C) 115 and 218 (D) 222 and 335

Look at the picture and answer the questions below.

Rectangle A

Rectangle B

15 Sarah wants to add rows or columns to the rectangle above and make 16 units. Which rectangle can she use? Rectangle A, B, or both?

(A) Rectangle A   (B) Rectangle B   (C) Both A and B rectangles

16 Jenny wants to add rows or columns to the rectangle above and make 20 units. Which rectangle can she use? Rectangle A, B, or both?

(A) Rectangle A   (B) Rectangle B   (C) Both A and B rectangles

2.4 Chapter Review

17 Linda wants to add rows to the rectangle above and make 25 units. Which rectangle should she use? Rectangle A, B, or both?

(A) Rectangle A   (B) Rectangle B   (C) Both A and B rectangles

18 Aaron wants to add columns to the rectangle above and make 21 units. Which rectangle should she uses, Rectangle A, B, or both?

(A) Rectangle A   (B) Rectangle B   (C) Both A and B rectangles

19 Johnny drew a rectangle with 5 rows and 7 columns. How many units are in his rectangle?

(A) 15 units   (B) 20 units   (C) 30 units   (D) 35 units

20 Becky partitioned a rectangle into 6 columns. She wants to make 42 units. How many rows does she need to make?

(A) 6 rows   (B) 2 rows   (C) 4 rows   (D) 7 rows

Next Chapter: Numbers and Operations In Base Ten

CHAPTER 3

NUMBERS AND OPERATIONS IN BASE TEN

PLACE VALUE UP TO THE THOUSANDTHS PLACE

Unit to 100

Place value is the numerical value that each digit in a number has.

Examples: ones place, tens place, hundreds place

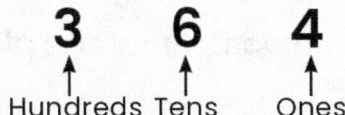

The number shown above is 364. The number 4 is in the ones place. The 6 is in the tens place. The 3 is in the hundreds place. This means that this number is made up of 4 groups of one, 6 groups of ten, and 3 groups of one hundred.

We can use base ten blocks to help understand place value.

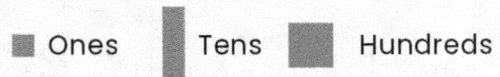

We can use these base ten blocks to make the number we used above.

PLACE VALUE UP TO THE THOUSANDTHS PLACE

Place Value Units to 1000

Place value is the numerical value that each digit in a number has.

Example: ones place, tens place, hundreds place

1 6 5 9

Thousands Hundreds Tens Ones

The number shown above is 1,659. The number 9 is in the ones place. The number 5 is in the tens place. The number 6 is in the hundreds place. The number 1 is in the thousands place.

We can use base ten blocks to represent this number.

■ Ones   ▌Tens   ■ Hundreds   ◈ Thousands

Place value is the numerical value that each digit in a number has. We can use base ten blocks to represent this number.

Place Value Up to the Thousandths Place

3.1

1 Write how many ones, tens, and hundreds are in the number 252

_____   _____   _____
HUNDREDS   TENS   ONES

2 Write how many ones, tens, and hundreds are in the number 30

_____   _____   _____
HUNDREDS   TENS   ONES

3 Write the number that goes along with the picture of base ten blocks.

4 Write the number that goes along with the picture of base ten blocks.

3.1 Place Value Up to the Thousandths Place

5 Use the space provided to draw your own picture using base ten blocks of the number given 210.

_____

6 Use the space provided to draw your own picture using base ten blocks of the number given 112.

_____

Use pictures with base ten blocks to help you solve the problems.

7 James is checking Cynthia's notebook during math class. Cynthia has 2 one blocks, 3 tens blocks, and 0 hundreds of blocks on her desk. What number has Cynthia made?

_____

8 Julie has 5 one's block, 1 tens of blocks, 8 hundreds of blocks, and 7 thousand of blocks on her desk. What number does this represent?

_____

9 There are 9874 people at a volleyball game. What number is in the thousand's place? What number is in the hundreds place? What number is in the tens place? What number is in the ones place?

_____

10 Chris and Sieana get 2388 the answer to their math problem. What number is in the thousand place? What number is in the hundreds place? What number is in the tens place? What number is in the ones place?

_____

11 Jennifer and Harris want to combine their stacks of cups. Jennifer has 2 stacks of one hundred cups, 3 stacks of ten cups, and 5 other cups. Harris has 4 stacks of one hundred cups, 6 stacks of ten cups, and 2 other cups. How many cups will they have together?

(A) 885   (B) 697   (C) 238   (D) 734

3.1 **Place Value Up to the Thousandths Place**

12 Peter drew this picture on his whiteboard.

Sherley drew this picture on her whiteboard.

If they combine their pictures together, what number will their picture represent?

(A) 5486   (B) 1486   (C) 2385   (D) 4565

13 Chris draws this picture on his paper.

Shiny drew this picture on his paper.

If they combine their pictures, what number will their picture represent?

(A) 2433   (B) 1586   (C) 7569   (D) 4221

**Place Value Up to
the Thousandths Place** **3.1**

14 Benny has 2 groups of one thousand scarves, 3 groups of one hundred scarves, 32 groups of ten scarfs, and 1 another scarf. How many scarves does Benny have?

(A) 2621   (B) 3261   (C) 3261   (D) 1452

15 Clue #1 - The mystery number is a 4-digit number.

Clue #2 - The digit in the thousands place is more than 5, but less than 7.

Clue #3 - The digit in the hundreds and tens place is the same.

Clue #4 - The digit in the tens place is 2 more than 1.

Clue #5 - The digit in the ones place is half of 10.

What is the mystery number?

(A) 6335   (B) 6553   (C) 5668   (D) 6334

16 Write how many ones, tens, and hundreds are in the number 823

HUNDREDS	TENS	ONES

17 Write how many ones, tens, and hundreds are in the number 1224

THOUSANDS	HUNDREDS	TENS	ONES

3.1

**Place Value Up to
the Thousandths Place**

18 Use the space provided to draw your own picture using base ten blocks of the number given 20.

_____

19 Use the space provided to draw your own picture using base ten blocks of the number given 1000.

_____

20 Becky is showing her teacher how she represented a number using base ten blocks. She used 6 one's blocks, 5 tens blocks, and 8 hundred blocks. What number did she represent with her base ten blocks?

(A) 835　　　(B) 856　　　(C) 865　　　(D) 658

Next Section: Expanded Form and Number Names

EXPANDED FORM AND NUMBER NAMES

Expanded Form

Expanded form is a way of writing a number in an equation form where the value of each digit is represented on its own.

$$7 \quad 4$$

Tens Ones

Numbers can also be represented in expanded form.

$$70 + 4 = 74$$

This number is 74. The digit in the ones place is 4. The value of that digit is 4 because 4 groups of one is 4. The digit in the tens place is 7. The value of that digit is 70 because 7 groups of ten is 70.

EXPANDED FORM AND NUMBER NAMES

Number Names

Number names is a way to write numbers in a written form with words that represent each place value.

Ones	Tens	Tens	Hundreds
1 -one	11- eleven	10- ten	100- one hundred
2- two	12- twelve	20- twenty	200- two hundred
3- three	13- thirteen	30- thirty	300- three hundred
4- four	14- fourteen	40- forty	400- four hundred
5- five	15- fifteen	50- fifty	500- five hundred
6- six	16- sixteen	60- sixty	600- six hundred
7- seven	17- seventeen	70- seventy	700- seven hundred
8- eight	18- eighteen	80- eighty	800- eight hundred
9- nine	19- nineteen	90- ninety	900- nine hundred

Thousands

1,000- one thousand	4,000- four thousand	7,000- seven thousand
2,000- two thousand	5,000- five thousand	8,000- eight thousand
3,000- three thousand	6,000- six thousand	9,000- nine thousand

You can use these words to write the number name form of a number. You write the words left to right in the same way the digits are written left to right.

629 = six hundred twenty-nine

Expanded Form and Number Names | 3.2

1 Fill in the part(s) missing from the expanded forms of these numbers. 80 + 5 = _____.

(A) 85

(B) 90

(C) 82

(D) 75

2 Fill in the part(s) missing from the expanded form of these numbers. 770 + 20 + 3 = _____.

(A) 773

(B) 793

(C) 800

(D) 750

3 Write the expanded form of the number. 95

(A) 90+5

(B) 90+2

(C) 89+5

(D) 96+3

4 Write the expanded form of the number. 880

(A) 800+70+50

(B) 700+20+60

(C) 800+60+20

(D) 600+80+90

5 A number has 2 hundreds, 5 tens, and 3 ones. Write the expanded form of this number.

(A) 200+60+5=265

(B) 200+60+3=263

(C) 200+50+3=253

(D) 200+40+5=245

3.2   **Expanded Form and Number Names**

6   Write the expanded form of the number. 7890

(A) 7005+500+30+60=7890   (B) 7000+800+30+50=7890

(C) 7010+800+33+50=7890   (D) 7000+800+90+0=7890

7 Daniel and Rebecca have 5 piles of one hundred chocolates, 2 piles of ten chocolates, and 7 other chocolates. How many chocolates do they have? Write the expanded form of that number.

(A) 500+20+7=527   (B) 500+30+5=557

(C) 500+40+3=553   (D) 500+70+2=572

8 Rambo is working on this expanded form problem. _____ + 200 + _____ + _____ = 4295. What numbers are missing from the equation? Explain how Rambo can figure out what numbers are missing.

(A) 2000+200+57+7=4295   (B) 3000+200+50+5=4295

(C) 4000+200+90+5=4295   (D) 4000+200+80+10=4295

Expanded Form and Number Names | **3.2**

9 Tim has 5 boxes of ten bats, 8 boxes of one hundred bats, and 2 other bats. How many bats does Tim have? Write the expanded form of this number.

(A) 800+50+2=852

(B) 800+50+2=885

(C) 800+50+2=862

(D) 800+50+2=888

10 Victor and Julia mix together their peanuts. Victor has 1 thousands, 4 hundreds, 2 tens, and 5 ones. Julia has 3 thousands, 2 hundreds, 6 tens, and 2 ones. How many pieces of peanuts do they have together? Write this number in expanded form.

(A) 4531 (B) 2333 (C) 4687 (D) 5695

11 Fill in the missing word

455 = four hundred _____ five.

(A) thirty (B) forty (C) twenty (D) fifty

12 Fill in the missing word(s)

6,789 = _____ seven hundred _____ nine

(A) five thousand/twenty

(B) five thousand/seventy

(C) six thousand/eighty

(D) two thousand/thirty

3.2   **Expanded Form and Number Names**

13 Write the number that goes along with the number name.

Five thousand two hundred fifty-six = _____

(A) 4569   (B) 5256   (C) 5366   (D) 3356

14 Write the number name for the number shown. 9854

(A) Nine thousand eight hundred fifty-four

(B) Nine thousand eight hundred fifty

(C) Nine thousand eight hundred fifty-six

(D) Nine thousand eight hundred sixty

15 Jane has 2 stacks of ten doughnuts and 5 other doughnuts. How many doughnuts does she have?

(A) Twenty- seven   (B) Fifty- two   (C) Twenty- five   (D) Thirty- five

16 Carmel and Jenny organize books into 5 stacks of one thousand books, 7 stacks of one hundred books, 2 stacks of ten books, and 1 other books. How many Books do they have?

(A) Five thousand four hundred fifty-three

(B) Five thousand seven hundred twenty-one

(C) Five thousand five hundred thirty

(D) Five thousand twenty-three

Expanded Form and Number Names | 3.2

17 Bruce and Alen want to combine their toys. Bruce has 4 piles of one hundred toys, 2 piles of ten toys, and 6 other toys. Alen has 3 piles of one hundred toys, 5 piles of ten toys, and 1 other toy. How many toys do they have together?

(A) Four hundred fifty-three

(B) Five hundred fifty-seven

(C) Seven hundred seventy-seven

(D) Six hundred fifty-seven

18 Annie wants to mix her pieces of cheese and her pieces of chocolate. She has 5 thousand, 6 hundreds, 3 tens, and 1 another piece of cheese. She has 3 thousands, 2 hundreds, 3 tens, and 5 other pieces of chocolates. How many pieces of cheese does she have?

(A) Five thousand three hundred fifty-five

(B) Eight thousand eight hundred twenty-five

(C) Eight thousand five hundred thirty

(D) Eight thousand eight hundred sixty-six

3.2   **Expanded Form and Number Names**

19 Siena is working on a physics problem. Five thousand _____ thirty - two = 5632. What is missing from the number name? Explain how siena can figure out what is missing.

- (A) Five hundred
- (B) Six Hundred
- (C) Three Hundred
- (D) Eight Hundred

20 A number has 2 ones, 6 tens, 3 hundreds, and 8 thousands. Choose the number name for the number.

- (A) Eight thousand sixty-five
- (B) Eight thousand three hundred sixty-two
- (C) Eight thousand seven hundred sixty-three
- (D) Eight thousand two hundred sixty

Next Section: Mental Math with 10s and 100s ≫

MENTAL MATH WITH 10S AND 100S

Mental Math with 10's

Mental math is math that you can do in your head.

You can use mental math to add 10 to any number. You just need to add one to the number in the tens place. The rest of the number will stay the same.

$$40 + 10 = 50$$
$$4 + 1 = 5$$

The original number was 40. There is a 4 in the tens place, so you add 1 to 4 (4+1), which equals 5. The rest of the number stays the same. This makes the answer 50.

Mental Math with 100's

Mental math is math that you can do in your head.

You can use mental math to add 100 to any number. You just need to add one to the number in the hundreds place. The rest of the number will stay the same.

$$400 + 100 = 500$$
$$4 + 1 = 5$$

The original number was 400. There is a 4 in the hundreds place, so you add 1 to 4 (4+1), which equals 5. The rest of the number stays the same. This makes the answer 500.

3.3 | **Mental Math with 10s and 100s**

Use mental math to solve the problems.

1 Alice has 30 apples and her mother gave 5 extra apples. How many apples does Alice have?

(A) 40   (B) 35   (C) 45   (D) 25

2 Lavina has 678 bags and she gave 6 bags to a poor man. How many bags does Lavina have remaining? 678 − 6 = _____.

(A) 672   (B) 650   (C) 662   (D) 670

3 Use mental math to add 10 to the number 568.

(A) 578   (B) 588   (C) 558   (D) 598

4 Use mental math to subtract 10 from the number 847.

(A) 854   (B) 844   (C) 837   (D) 827

5 Fionna has 40 boxes. She gets 10 more boxes.
How many boxes does she have now?

(A) 30   (B) 40   (C) 50   (D) 70

6 Jane has 280 pencils. She gives 10 of them away.
How many pencils does Jane have now?

(A) 250   (B) 270   (C) 290   (D) 260

7 Tina and Tim make 707 cupcakes. They give 10 to their friends. How many cupcakes do they have left?

(A) 710   (B) 697   (C) 717   (D) 703

8 Use mental math to solve the problem.
890 – 890 = _____.

(A) 1   (B) 10   (C) 100   (D) 0

9 Roger has 559 pipes. Jerry has 10 more pipes than Roger. How many pipes does Jerry have?

(A) 857   (B) 569   (C) 669   (D) 549

10 Use mental math to solve the problem. 1117 – 10 = _____.

(A) 118   (B) 1127   (C) 1107   (D) 1111

3.3   **Mental Math with 10s and 100s**

11   Use mental math to solve the problem. 505 + 100 = _____.

A) 515   B) 615   C) 605   D) 650

12   Use mental math to solve the problem. 798 – 100 = _____.

A) 788   B) 698   C) 598   D) 898

13   Use mental math to add 100 to the number 547.

A) 447   B) 347   C) 647   D) 747

14   Linda has 980 baskets. She gets 100 more. How many baskets does she have now?

A) 1080   B) 1180   C) 880   D) 980

15   David has 777 clips. He loses 100 of them. How many clips does he have now?

A) 677   B) 667   C) 877   D) 887

16   Use mental math to solve the problem. 2009+100= _____

A) 2119   B) 2109   C) 2209   D) 2229

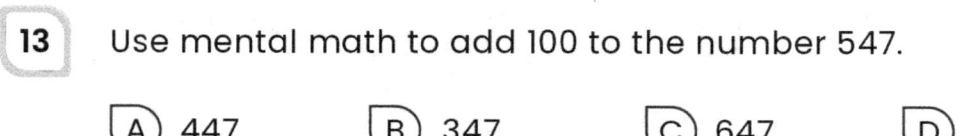

Mental Math with 10s and 100s | 3.3

17 Use mental math to solve the problem 7435 – 100 = _____.

(A) 7335   (B) 6335   (C) 7425   (D) 7235

18 Robert has 555 bottles. He buys 100 more from Rubina. How many bottles does Robert have now?

(A) 565   (B) 655   (C) 755   (D) 455

19 Tiny has 800 pounds. Mensa has 100 pounds less than Tiny. How many pounds does Mensa have?

(A) 700   (B) 900   (C) 600   (D) 800

20 There are 10000 people at a stadium. 100 people leave the stadium. How many people are still at the stadium?

(A) 9900   (B) 10100   (C) 9999   (D) 9000

Next Section:
Comparing Numbers

COMPARING NUMBERS

Comparing numbers is examining numbers to see if one number is greater than the other number, one number is less than the other number, or if both numbers are equal.

These are the symbols you can use when comparing numbers.

> **greater than**   < **less than**   = **equal to**

Think of the greater than and less than signs as an alligator mouth. Alligators like to eat a lot of food, so the alligator mouth is always going to open up toward the bigger number.

27 < 46

The two numbers being compared are 27 and 46. You have to decide which symbol to write in the middle of the two numbers. 27 is not bigger than 46, so you cannot use the greater than symbol. The two numbers are not the same, so you cannot use the equal to symbol. 46 is bigger than 27, so you have to use the less than symbol. This means that the alligator's mouth is opening up toward the bigger number (46).

483 > 431

The two numbers being compared are 483 and 431. The greater than symbol was placed between the two numbers because 483 is bigger than 431. The alligator's mouth is opening up toward the bigger number (483).

625 = 625

The two numbers being compared are 625 and 625. The equal to symbol was placed between the two numbers because both numbers are the same. They are equal to each other.

Comparing Numbers 3.4

1 Write whether the correct or incorrect symbol is used. 57 = 55.

Ⓐ Correct Ⓑ Incorrect

2 Write whether the correct or incorrect symbol is used. 575 < 615.

Ⓐ Correct Ⓑ Incorrect

3 Write whether the correct or incorrect symbol is used. 950 > 1000.

Ⓐ Correct Ⓑ Incorrect

4 Write the correct symbol in the middle of the two numbers
170 _____ 155.

Ⓐ > Ⓑ < Ⓒ = Ⓓ None of the above

5 Write the correct symbol in the middle of the two numbers
765 _____ 765.

Ⓐ > Ⓑ <

Ⓒ = Ⓓ None of the above

3.4   Comparing Numbers

6   Write the correct symbol in the middle of the two numbers
345_____355.

(A) >   (B) <   (C) =   (D) None of the above

7   Chris is working on this math problem. 675_____689
What symbol should Chris use to correctly answer the question?

(A) >   (B) <   (C) =   (D) None of the above

8   Daisy sees this comparing numbers problem on her homework. 517_____500. What symbol should she use to correctly answer the question?

(A) >   (B) <

(C) =   (D) None of the above

9   Lauren has bought 566 apples. Clady also bought an equal number of apples. How many apples did Clady buy? Choose the comparing number equation below using the two numbers and the correct symbol.

(A) 566 > 566   (B) 566 < 566   (C) 566 = 566

Comparing Numbers | 3.4

10 Jerry ate 140 dates. Benny ate a greater number of dates than Jerry. How many dates do you think Benny ate?

(A) A number greater than 140. (B) A number less than 140.

(C) 140 (D) 150

11 Tyron has 720 cookies. Mike has 735 cookies. Choose the comparing number equation below using the two numbers and the correct symbol.

(A) 720 > 735 (B) 720 < 735 (C) 720 = 735 (D) 721 = 735

12 Mr. Brigenza is discussing this problem with his class. 590 > 690. They are deciding if it is correct or incorrect.
Do you think it is correct or incorrect? Why do you think this?
If it is incorrect, what would you do to fix it?

(A) Correct (B) Incorrect

13 Write the correct symbol in the middle of the two numbers to correctly compare the numbers. 1564 _____ 1555.

(A) > (B) < (C) = (D) None of the above

3.4   **Comparing Numbers**

14 Write the correct symbol in the middle of the two numbers to correctly compare the numbers.

300 + 50 + 3 _____ 500 + 20 + 2.

(A) >   (B) <   (C) =   (D) None of the above

15 Rachel saw 150 dogs on the highway. Tom saw 190 dogs on the highway. Choose the comparing number equation below using the two numbers and the correct symbol.

(A) 150 > 190   (B) 150 < 190   (C) 150 = 190   (D) 150 = 191

16 Write the correct symbol in the middle of the two numbers to correctly compare the numbers.

9722 _____ 9722.

(A) >   (B) <   (C) =   (D) None of the above

17 Write the correct symbol in the middle of the two numbers to correctly compare the numbers.

515 + 15 +2 _____ 517 + 25 + 5.

(A) >   (B) <   (C) =   (D) None of the above

Comparing Numbers 3.4

18 Write the correct symbol in the middle of the two numbers to correctly compare the numbers.

Five hundred fifteen _____ Five hundred fifty-one.

(A) >   (B) <   (C) =   (D) None of the above

19 Write the correct symbol in the middle of the two numbers to correctly compare the numbers.

500 + 40 + 5 _____ 480 + 55 + 10.

(A) >   (B) <   (C) =   (D) None of the above

20 Write the correct symbol in the middle of the two numbers to correctly compare the numbers.

Six hundred Thirty-three _____ Six hundred sixty-three1.

(A) >   (B) <   (C) =   (D) None of the above

Next Section: Chapter Review

3.5 Chapter Review

1 Draw a picture using base ten blocks to represent 3221.

2 What number do these base ten blocks represent?

A) 2445   B) 2434   C) 3434   D) 5454

Use pictures of base ten blocks to help you solve the problem.

3 Rebecca has 2 ones blocks, 6 tens blocks, 4 hundreds blocks, and 5 thousands blocks on her desk. What number does this represent?

A) 2456   B) 2645   C) 5462   D) 5265

4 There are 1004 people at the department store. 100 more people walk into the store. How many people are at the store now? Use mental math to solve the problem.

(A) 994 (B) 1114 (C) 1104 (D) 1014

5 Kim and Robert have 5 stacks of ten books, 6 stacks of one thousand books, 8 other books, and 9 stacks of one hundred books. How many books do they have?

(A) 6000+900+50+8=6958 (B) 5000+600+80+5=5685

(C) 6000+500+90+8=6958 (D) 9000+600+50+8=9658

6 Dan and Raquel have 5 piles of one hundred diamonds, 2 piles of ten diamonds, and 5 other diamonds. How many diamonds do they have?

(A) 500+20+5=525 (B) 200+50+5=255

(C) 500+50+5=555 (D) 500+30+5=535

7 Charles has 555 flowers. He plucks 100 more flowers. How many flowers does Charles have now? Use mental math to solve the problem.

(A) 566 (B) 655 (C) 656 (D) 577

3.5   Chapter Review

8 Rose saw 8 piles of one thousand plates, 4 piles of one hundred plates, 3 piles of ten plates, and 9 other plates. How many plates did Rose see?

(A) 8439   (B) 4839   (C) 3984   (D) 9843

Use mental math to add or subtract 10 to solve the problem.

---

9 Carlos has 790 blocks. He got 10 more blocks. How many blocks does Carlos have?

(A) 780   (B) 800   (C) 810   (D) 760

10 Tomy has 10000 crackers. He buys 100 more from Jenilia. How many crackers does Tomy have now?

(A) 10100   (B) 11110   (C) 9000   (D) 9900

11 Roger has 110 pieces of paper. He gives 10 to his brother. How many does he have left?

(A) 100   (B) 90   (C) 120   (D) 80

12 Shirley has 905 candles. Melissa has 100 candles less than Shirley. How many candles does Melissa have?

(A) 705   (B) 805   (C) 1005   (D) 955

13 Jim is working on a math problem. Nine thousand _____ fifty five = 9855. What is missing from the number name? Explain how Jim can figure out what is missing.

(A) Five hundred

(B) Six Hundred

(C) Three Hundred

(D) Eight Hundred

14 Peter has 5 groups of one thousand scarves, 8 groups of one hundred scarves, 28 groups of ten scarves, and 1 another scarf. How many scarves does Peter have?

(A) 5838

(B) 8528

(C) 5828

(D) 2958

15 There are 8 piles of one hundred bundles, 3 piles of ten bundles, and 7 other bundles. How many bundles are there?

(A) 800+30+7=837

(B) 500+30+7=537

(C) 800+70+3=873

(D) 500+70+3=573

16 Choose the expanded form of the number 697

(A) 600+90+7=697

(B) 900+60+7=697

(C) 700+60+3=697

(D) 500+90+3=697

3.5   **Chapter Review**

17   What number do these base ten blocks represent?

- (A) 57
- (B) 75
- (C) 55
- (D) 65

18   Use mental math to add or subtract 10 to solve the problem.
Andes has 57 English books and gives 10 books to his friend. How many books does Andes have?

- (A) 67
- (B) 45
- (C) 47
- (D) 52

19   Draw a picture using base ten blocks to represent 311.

20   There are 9 piles of one thousand bottles, 1 pile of one hundred bottles, 5 piles of ten bottles, and 3 other bottles. How many bottles are there?

- (A) Nine thousand one hundred and fifty-three
- (B) One thousand nine hundred and fifty-five
- (C) Five thousand one hundred and thirty-five
- (D) Nine thousand two hundred and fifty-three

Next Chapter:
Measurement And Data

CHAPTER 4

MEASUREMENT AND DATA

HELP THE BEES GET TO THE HIVE!

MEASURING LENGTH IN STANDARD UNITS AND METRIC UNITS

Measuring Length in Standard Units

There are two different units of measurement used to measure the length (how tall or long) of something: the standard unit of measurement and the metric unit of measurement. In this lesson we will be working with the standard unit of measurement. The standard unit of measurement includes inches, feet, and yards.

An inch is about as long as a small paper clip.

A foot is 12 inches long (12 small paper clips long). A foot is about as tall as a large (2 liter) bottle of soda.

A yard is 3 feet long (3 large bottles of soda long). A yard is about as long as a guitar.

A ruler can be used to measure inches and one foot. There are 2 sides of a ruler. One side can be used to measure in inches. On this side of the ruler the numbers go from 0 to 12. The other side of the ruler can be used to measure in centimeters (in the metric unit of measurement). On this side of the ruler the numbers go from 0 to 30.

A yardstick can be used to measure feet and one yard.

A measuring tape can be used to measure longer/taller objects in feet and yards.

To measure an object line it up at the 0 on the ruler, yardstick, or measuring tape.

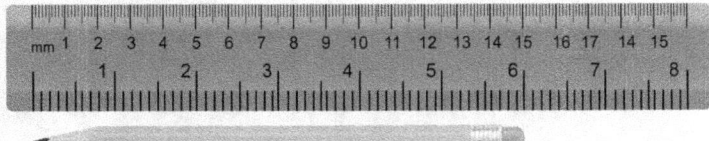

The tip of the pencil is lined up at the 0 on the ruler. The eraser on the pencil lines up at the 6 on the ruler. This means the pencil is 6 inches long.

MEASURING LENGTH IN STANDARD UNITS AND METRIC UNITS

Measuring Length in Metric Units

The metric unit of measurement includes meters and centimeters.

A centimeter is about as long as a staple. We can write centimeters as cm.

A meter is 100 centimeters long, which is about as long as a guitar. We can write meters as m.

A ruler can be used to measure centimeters. There are 2 sides of a ruler. One side can be used to measure in inches. On this side of the ruler the numbers go from 0 to 12. The other side of the ruler can be used to measure in centimeters. On this side of the ruler the numbers go from 0 to 30.

A meter stick can be used to measure centimeters and a meter.

A measuring tape can be used to measure longer/taller objects in centimeters and meters.

To measure an object line, it up at the 0 on the ruler, yardstick, or measuring tape.

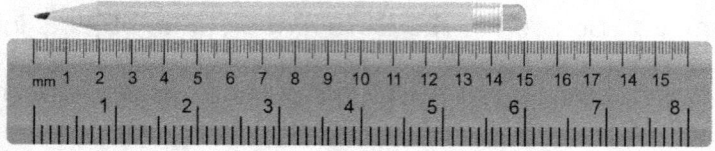

The tip of the pencil is lined up at the 0 on the ruler. The eraser on the pencil lines up at the 15 on the ruler. This means the pencil is 15 centimeters long.

Decide which measurement tool would be the best to measure the length of an object.

1 Length of a Candle

(A) Ruler   (B) Yardstick   (C) Measuring Tape

2 Height of a Pencil

(A) Ruler   (B) Yardstick   (C) Measuring Tape

3 Width of a Sticky Note

(A) Ruler   (B) Yardstick   (C) Measuring Tape

4 Height of a Tree

(A) Ruler   (B) Yardstick   (C) Measuring Tape

5 Use a ruler to measure how many inches in length the objects are. If the object does not exactly line up with one of the inches on your ruler, choose the inch length it is closest to. A pen is _____ inches long.

6 Sherin is measuring how wide the nightstand in his room is. What measurement tool should he use?

_____

7 Linda and Mary are measuring how long the path in their backyard is. Linda thinks they should use a ruler. Mary thinks they should use a measuring tape. Who is correct? Why do you think they are correct?

_____

8 A rose plant measures 15 centimeters tall. The next week it measures 25 centimeters tall. How many centimeters did the rose plant grow over the week?

(A) 10   (B) 15   (C) 25   (D) 16

9 Jennifer wants to measure the length of her trailer. She does not have a meter stick or a measuring tape. She only has a ruler. Use words and pictures to explain how Jennifer could use a ruler to measure the length of the trailer.

_____

10 Mary and her sister Becky want to measure how wide a chip is. Mary wants to use a yardstick. Becky wants to use a ruler. Who is correct? Why do you think they are correct?

_____

11 Isaac and Lisa are measuring the height of the wall in their back room. Isaac says the wall is 3 meters tall. Lisa says the wall is 300 centimeters tall. Their mom tells them they are both correct. Why are they both correct?

_____

12 Kinston is 55 inches tall. Her older brother Gaston is 12 inches taller than Kinston. How tall is Gaston?

Ⓐ 60 inches   Ⓑ 67 inches   Ⓒ 50 inches   Ⓓ 52 inches

13 Robert has 3 pieces of strips. He wants to see how long they will be if he lays them on the floor in a line. The yellow piece of the strip is 31 inches long. The blue piece of the strip is 25 inches long. The Red piece of the strip is 40 inches long. How long are all of the pieces of strips put together?

Ⓐ 60 inches   Ⓑ 80 inches   Ⓒ 96 inches   Ⓓ 76 inches

MEASUREMENT AND DATA

4.1 Measuring Length in Standard Units and Metric Units

14 Kenny and Lavinia measure the width of a table. Kenny says it is 200 cm wide. Lavinia says it is 2 meters wide. Their teacher tells them they are both correct. Why are they both correct?

_____

15 Nancy measures the length of a spaghetti noodle. She finds that it is 14 inches long. Her friend Olivia also measures the same spaghetti noodle. She finds that it is 1 foot long. Did they get the same measurement? Explain your thinking.

_____

16 Bob has a beige piece of construction paper that is 48 inches wide and a tan piece of construction paper that is 4 feet wide. Which piece of construction paper is wider, or are they the same width? Explain your thinking.

_____

17 Allen is trying to measure how tall a mixing bowl is. He does not have a ruler or a measuring tape. He only has a meter stick. Use words and pictures to explain how Allen could use a meter stick to measure the height of the mixing bowl.

_____

18 Palona's backyard is 3157 inches wide. Her neighbor's yard is 3365 inches wide. How wide are their two backyards put together?

(A) 5622 inches

(B) 4527 inches

(C) 6522 inches

(D) 6122 inches

19 Martin's farm is 2826 meters wide. Rosy's farm is 5263 meters wide. How wide are their two farms put together?

(A) 5622 meters

(B) 8089 meters

(C) 6522 meters

(D) 7520 meters

20 Pricy draws a red line on the sidewalk with chalk that is 4562 inches long. She also draws a yellow line with chalk. She drew a total of 6823 inches with chalk. How long was the yellow line Pricy drew?

(A) 2261 inches

(B) 2568 inches

(C) 3321 inches

(D) 2081 inches

Next Section: Comparing Lengths in Standard and Metric Units ≫

COMPARING LENGTHS IN STANDARD AND METRIC UNITS

There are two different units of measurement used to measure the length (how tall or long) of something: the standard unit of measurement and the metric unit of measurement. The standard unit of measurement includes inches, feet, and yards. The metric unit of measurementD includes meters and centimeters.

An object can be measured using both units of measurement. The length of the duck can be measured in inches and centimeters.

The duck is 7 inches long.   The duck is 17 centimeters long.

7 is a smaller number than 17, but they describe the same length just in different units.

1 Find an object to measure the width, length, or height of it. Use a ruler to measure these objects using inches and centimeters.

Object _____.

Length in Inches _____.

Length in centimeters _____.

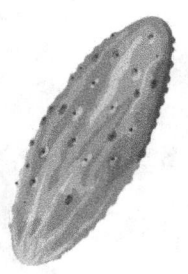

2 A cucumber is _____ wide.

(A) 10 inches (B) 10 cm (C) 10 feet (D) 10 meters

3 A broom is _____ tall.

(A) 8 inches (B) 8 cm (C) 8 feet (D) 8 yards

4 A shampoo bottle is _____ tall.

(A) 22 inches (B) 22 cm (C) 22 meters (D) 22 yards

5 The fish in the picture below is _____ long.

(A) 7 inches (B) 7 cm

(C) 7 meters (D) 7 yards

4.2 Comparing Lengths in Standard and Metric Units

6 The table is _____ tall.

(A) 12 staples

(B) 12 paperclips

(C) 12 loaves of bread

(D) 12 guitars

7 What is longer? 5 centimeters or 5 inches? Explain your thinking.

_____

8 What is shorter? 15 feet or 15 yards? Explain your thinking.

_____

9 Lisa thinks that her piece of cloth that is 2 yards long is shorter than her piece of cloth that is 8 inches long. Is she correct? Explain your thinking.

_____

10 Rachel thinks that 10 feet are longer than 8 feet because 10 is a larger number than 8. Is she correct? Explain your thinking.

_____

11 Aaron says that his farm house is 5 yards in length. Mack says that Aaron's farm is 5 feet. Who is correct? Explain your thinking.

_____

12 Mrs. Eliza asks her class how far they have to run in the race. Is it 100 centimeters, 100 inches, 100 feet, or 100 meters? What is the correct answer? Explain your thinking.

_____

13 What is longer? 550 meters or 550 inches? Explain your thinking.

_____

14 When you measure the length of an object using inches and centimeters, the number of centimeters will always be higher than the number of inches. Why is this true?.

_____

15 Bob's basket is 3 feet wide. John's basket is 45 centimeters wide. Whose basket is wider, or are they the same width? Explain your thinking.

_____

16 Is a donut 8 paper clips wide or 8 guitars wide? Which is correct? Explain your thinking.

_____

17 Why is 1 foot longer than 1 centimeter, even though they both have the number 1 in them?

_____

18 The airplane in the picture below is _____ long.

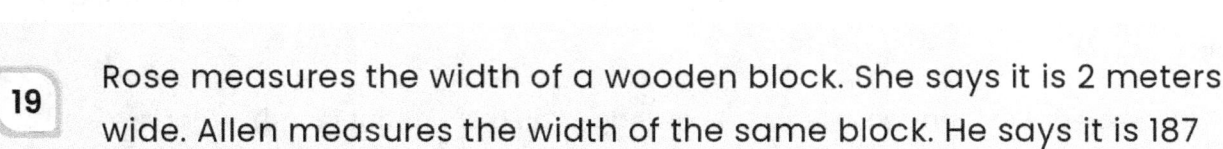

(A) 14 inches (B) 14 cm

(C) 14 meters (D) 14 yards

19 Rose measures the width of a wooden block. She says it is 2 meters wide. Allen measures the width of the same block. He says it is 187 centimeters wide. Did they get the same measurement?

_____

20 What is shorter? 10 centimeters or 10 feet? Explain your thinking.

_____

Next Section: Estimating Lengths ≫

ESTIMATING LENGTHS

Estimating length is making a smart guess about how long, wide, or tall something is.

When you are estimating, use your knowledge you have about length. What are things that are about a centimeter, meter, inch, or foot long? Use this to help you decide what measurements would be best to measure an object. Also, use that knowledge to help you decide how many units long, wide, or tall an object is. Estimations are not perfect measurements, but they give an idea of how long, wide, or tall something is.

How long is a car?

A car is a large object, so it would not make sense to measure it in centimeters or inches. They are too small. You could measure it in either feet or meters.

4 meters or 12 feet

Using your knowledge of measurement, you could come up with the estimations above. Everyone's estimations will not be exactly the same, but they will be close.

Choose which unit of measurement would be best to estimate the height of an object.

1 A grass

(A) Meters   (B) Feet   (C) Inches   (D) Centimeters

2 A Squirrel

(A) Meters   (B) Feet   (C) Inches   (D) Centimeters

Estimate the length, width, or height of the item.

3 How wide do you think a fig is?

(A) 4 Meters   (B) 4 Feet   (C) 4 Inches   (D) 4 Centimeters

4 How long do you think a bat is?

(A) 12 Meters   (B) 12 Feet   (C) 12 Inches   (D) 12 Centimeters

5 How long do you think a towel is?

(A) 5 Feet   (B) 15 feet   (C) 14 feet   (D) 25 feet

4.3   **Estimating Lengths**

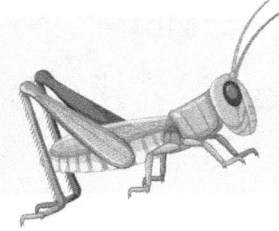

6   How long is a grasshopper? _____.

7   How long is a grain of rice? _____.

8   How wide is a mango? _____.

9   Mr. George wants to come up with something that is less than an inch wide. What is something that is less than an inch wide?

_____

10   Sarah's dad asks her to think of something that is a centimeter long. What is something that is a centimeter long?

_____

11 Why do you think it is useful to know how to estimate the length of something?

_____

Estimate the length, width, or height of the picture in inches or centimeters. Use a ruler to measure the actual length, width, or height of the picture. Find the difference in your estimated length, width, or height of the picture and the actual length, width, or height of the picture.

12 How wide do you think the penguin is? _____ inches

What is the actual width of the penguin? _____ inches

What is the difference in your estimated width and the actual width of the penguin?

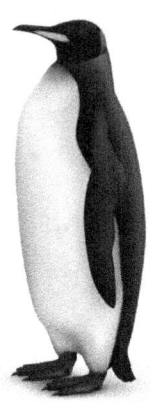

_____

13 How tall do you think the frog is? _____ inches

What is the actual height of the frog? _____ inches

What is the difference in your estimated height of the frog and the actual height of the frog?

_____

4.3   **Estimating Lengths**

14

How tall do you think the doughnut is?
_____ centimeters.

What is the actual height of the doughnut?
_____ centimeters.

What is the difference between your estimated length of the clock and the actual length of the doughnut?

_____

15   Estimate the length, width, or height of the item.

How long do you think a small insect is?

(A) 2 cm   (B) 15 cm   (C) 6 cm   (D) 10 cm

16   Mr. James estimates that the horse fence should be 8 feet tall. His neighbor Mr. Christopher estimates the fence should be is 15 feet tall. Who do you think made a better estimation? Explain your thinking.

_____

17   Ms. Robinson is trying to estimate the width of a stool. What unit of measurement could Ms. Robinson use to estimate the width of a stool?

_____

18 Estimate the length, width, or height of the items.

How wide is a glass? _____.

19 Ann is estimating the height of a tube light. What unit of measurement could Ann use to estimate the height of a tube light?

_____

20 Estimate the length, width, or height of the items. Use the unit of measurement given to estimate.

What is the height of a book?_____ inches

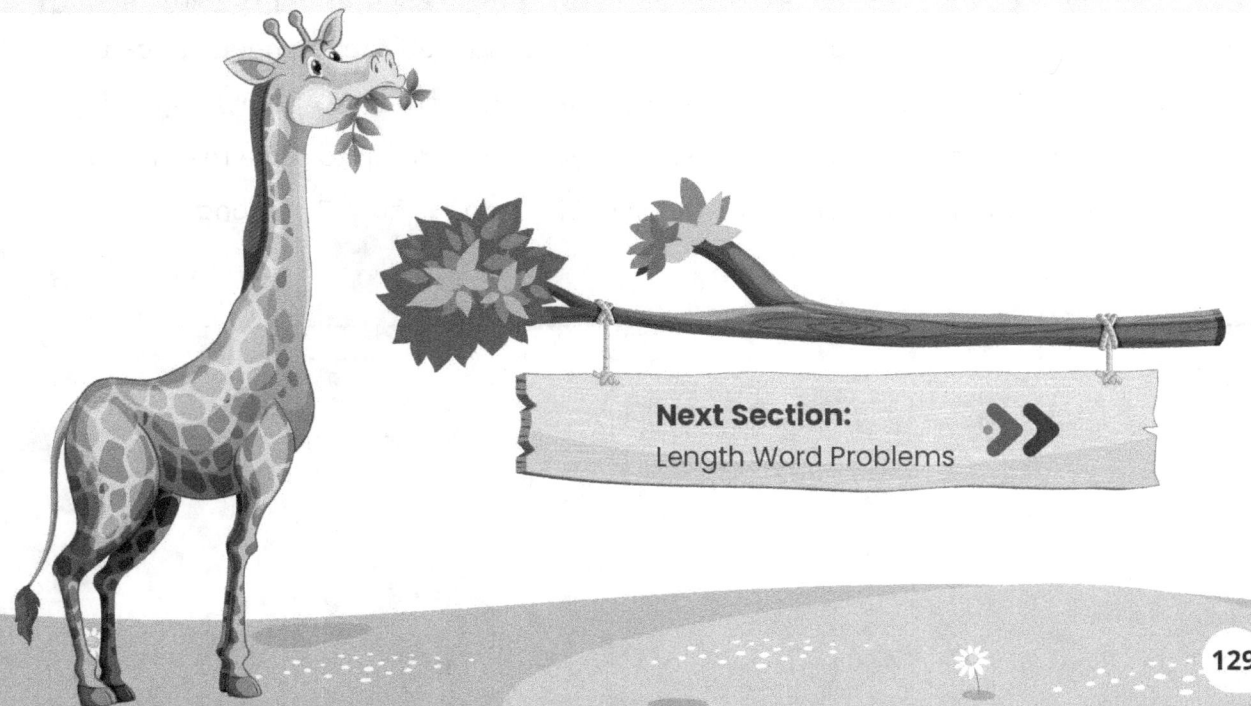

Next Section:
Length Word Problems

LENGTH WORD PROBLEMS

One and two step addition and subtraction word problems can involve length. You can solve them by making an equation or by drawing a picture.

Helen has a piece of string that is 30 cm long. She cuts 13 cm off of the string. How long is the piece of string now?

$$30 - 13 = ?$$

$$\begin{array}{r} \overset{2\ 10}{\cancel{30}} \\ -\ 13 \\ \hline 17 \end{array}$$

You can use the "make an equation strategy" to solve the word problem. After reading the word problem, you can determine that subtraction needs to be used because she cuts off some of the string. It is getting smaller. After writing the equation, it can be rewritten vertically, so you can regroup to solve the problem. When you subtract 13 from 30 it equals 17. The string is now 17 cm long.

LENGTH WORD PROBLEMS

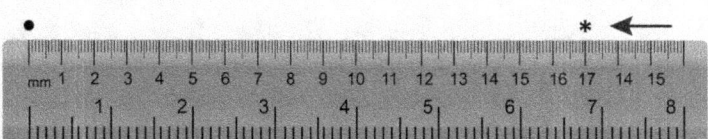

You can use the "draw a picture strategy" to solve the word problem by drawing a picture of a ruler. After reading the word problem, you can determine that subtraction needs to be used because she cuts off some of the string. You start by drawing a picture of a ruler. Mark a circle where the equation starts. In this word problem that is at 30, which is how long the string is to begin with. Since subtraction is being used, you move left on the number line toward smaller numbers. Move 13 numbers down the ruler because that is how many centimeters Helen cuts off. Put a star where you land on the ruler. In this problem that is at 17, which is the answer to the equation. The string is now 17 centimeters long.

These same strategies can be used to solve both steps in a two step word problem.

4.4 Length Word Problems

> Draw a picture of a ruler to help solve the addition problems with length.
> In addition move to the right (toward larger numbers on the ruler).

1 34 cm – 12 cm = _____ cm.

(A) 15 cm   (B) 22 cm   (C) 18 cm   (D) 10 cm

2 22 inches – 9 inches = _____ inches.

(A) 13 inches   (B) 18 inches   (C) 21 inches   (D) 11 inches

3 10 inches + 5 inches = _____ inches.

(A) 13 inches   (B) 15 inches   (C) 21 inches   (D) 11 inches

4 25 cm + 8 cm = _____ cm.

(A) 33 cm   (B) 22 cm

(C) 28 cm   (D) 36 cm

1 inch = 2.54 cm

Use the draw-a-picture strategy to solve the addition word problems.

5 Allen's pen is 10 cm tall. His Pencil is 3 cm taller than his pen. How many centimeters tall is his pencil?

(A) 12   (B) 13   (C) 15   (D) 17

6 Cindy has 3 books stacked on top of each other. Each book is 7 cm tall. How tall are the 3 books stacked together?

(A) 31   (B) 25   (C) 21   (D) 19

Use the make-an-equation strategy to solve the addition and subtraction word problems.

7 Benny has a drum that is 88 inches tall. His best friend Siena has a drum that is 13 inches shorter than Benny's. How tall is Siena's drum?

(A) 70   (B) 75   (C) 63   (D) 78

4.4   Length Word Problems

Use the make an equation and then draw picture strategies to solve the two-step word problems with addition and subtraction.

8 Lucy has 5 candies that she lines up on the counter. Each candy is 12 inches long.

Ⓐ How long are the 5 candies together? _____.

Ⓑ Lucy serves 24 inches of candies to her customers. How many inches of candies does she have left?

_____.

9 **Use the draw a picture strategy to solve the subtraction word problems.**

Gaynell has a piece of rope that is 42 cm long. She cuts off 8 cm of the rope. How long is the piece of rope now?

Ⓐ 33   Ⓑ 25   Ⓒ 34   Ⓓ 27

10 Hanford's table is 58 centimeters long. Amanda's table is 11 centimeters longer than Hanford's table.

Ⓐ How long is Amanda's table? _____
Becky's table is 8 centimeters shorter than Amanda's table.

Ⓑ How long is Becky's table? _____

Length Word Problems | 4.4

11 Tetley is buying foil at the hardware store. He is deciding between a foil that is 4 yards long and a foil that is 7 feet long. Both foils are the same price. Which foil should Tetley buy?

_____

12 The train track is 1056 feet long. They add 263 feet to the track. How long is the track now?

(A) 1563   (B) 1319   (C) 1756   (D) 1619

13 Maddy is buying wire at a store. She is deciding between a roll of wire that is 2 meter long and a roll of wire that is 180 centimeters long. Both rolls cost the same amount of money. Which roll of wire should Maddy buy?

_____

14 Stanley and Joshua make a sandwich that is 24 inches wide. They also make a cheese sandwich that is 8 inches wide. Their friends eat 6 inches of sandwiches. How much sandwiches do they have left?

_____

4.4   **Length Word Problems**

15 Use the make an equation strategy to solve the addition and subtraction word problems.

A tamarind tree is 33 inches tall. A year later the tree is 89 inches tall. How many inches did the tamarind tree grow over the course of the year?

A) 68   B) 56   C) 49   D) 79

16 Brian buys a rope that is 55 cm long. He adds another 9 cm to the rope. Then, he cuts 17 cm from the rope. How long is the rope that is left now?

_____

17 Ronald has a chain that is 230 centimeters long. He also has another chain that is 289 centimeters long. He hooks the chains together. How long are the 2 chains together?

A) 519   B) 630   C) 570   D) 489

18 Ryan weighs 83 lbs. Tim weighs 91 lbs. How much do Ryan and Tim weigh together?

A) 174   B) 156   C) 186   D) 145

19 Jason has a blanket that is 127 inches wide. Jason has a blanket that is 209 inches wide. What is the difference in the width of the blanket?

(A) 100   (B) 82   (C) 76   (D) 96

20 The sidewalk at the park is 613 feet long. They add 115 feet to the sidewalk. How long on the sidewalk now?

(A) 650   (B) 728   (C) 752   (D) 705

Next Section: Graphing and Data »

GRAPHING AND DATA

Bar Graph:

Data is information with numbers. A bar graph is a way to show data or information with numbers using bars on a graph to represent different numbers.

Mr. Jeffery asks his class what their favourite fruits are. 6 students said their favourite fruit was a banana. 12 students said their favourite fruit was a strawberry. 8 students said their favourite fruit was an apple. 3 students said their favourite fruit was an orange.

This information can be shown in a data table.

Favorite Fruits in Mr. Jeffery's Class

FRUIT	NUMBER OF STUDENTS
Banana	6
Strawberry	12
Apple	8
Orange	3

The same data can also be represented in a vertical bar graph. The height of each bar shows how many kids think that particular fruit is their favourite.

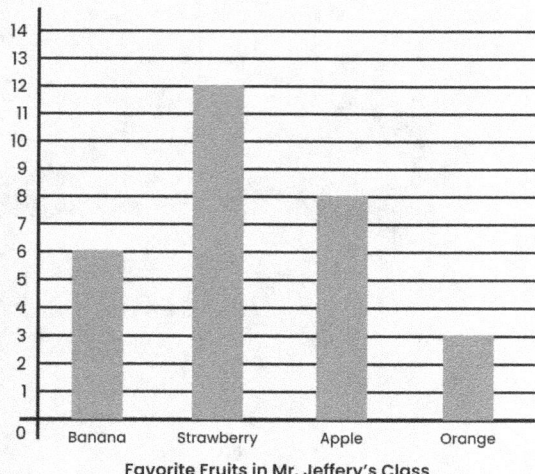

Favorite Fruits in Mr. Jeffery's Class

GRAPHING AND DATA

Line Graph:

Data can be collected using measurement. This can include the lengths, widths, and heights of objects. This type of data can be represented using a line plot. A line plot is a type of graph that marks points above a number line showing how many of each number are present.

The pencils in a box are 10 cm, 12 cm, 9 cm, 10 cm, 15 cm, 14 cm, 12 cm, 16 cm, 18 cm, 19 cm, and 11 cm.

This data can be represented in a line plot.

Lengths of Pencils

```
                X               X
    X           X       X       X               X       X       X                       X       X
   ─────────────────────────────────────────────────────────────────────────────────────────────
    9          10      11      12      13      14      15      16      17      18      19
```
X = 1 Pencil

Pictograph:

Data from a data table can be represented in a vertical pictograph. Each picture of a pencil represents 1 pencil. The pictures in a pictograph can be related to what is being represented in the graph.

How many pencils are on their desks?

John	●	●		
Jennifer	●	●	●	●
Emily				
Tage	●			

● = 1 Pencil

4.5   **Graphing and Data**

1 Ava could create a picture graph for different types of fruits by her house. There are 16 oranges and 8 apples.

Fruits by Ava house

Strawberries	●	●
Bananas	●	●
Apples		
Oranges		

● = 4 Fruits

How would you draw the number of oranges and apples in this picture graph?

_____

2 Use the line plot.

Height of clocks

```
                    X
  X                 X              X              X
  X     X           X              X              X
  ─────────────────────────────────────────────────
  12    13    14    15    16    17    18    19    20
```

X = 1 Clock

How many more clocks are 15 inches tall than 18 inches tall?

_____.

3 Use the horizontal bar graph below to answer the question.

Favorite type of Pizza

Cheese	● ● ● ●
Pepperoni	● ● ● ●
Sausage	● ●
Veggie	●

● = 3 People

How many people chose cheese as their favorite type of pizza?

_____

4 Emma is studying for her math class and analyzing a bar graph that shows the number of apple pies and key lime pies at a bake sale. She wants to know the difference between the number of apple pies and key lime pies. How many more apple pies are there than key lime pies at the bake sale?

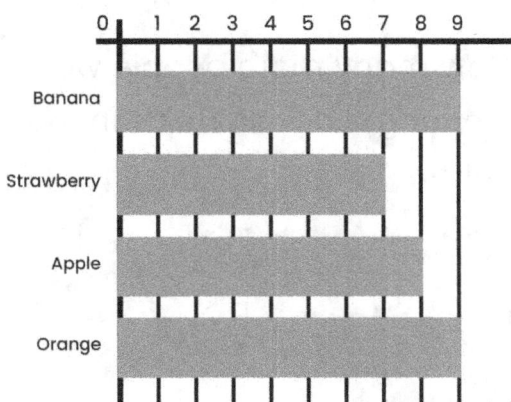

Types of Pies at the Bake Sale

A) 1   B) 2

C) 3   D) 5

4.5 Graphing and Data

5 Ava could create a picture graph for different types of fruits by her house. There are 16 oranges and 8 apples.

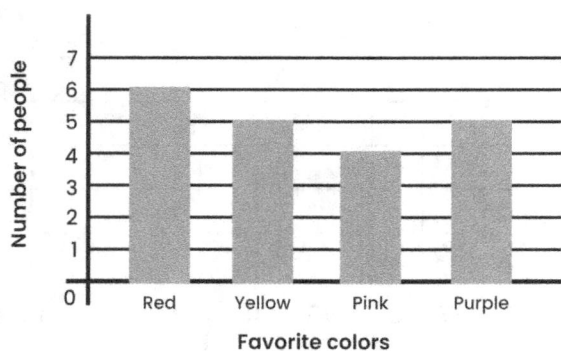

How many more students like red and purple than pink and yellow?

(A) 11 (B) 2 (C) 9 (D) 3

6 Megan created a vertical bar graph that displays the number of people wearing different colored shirts at the park. What does the vertical bar graph tell us about the distribution of shirt colors at the park?

How many more people were wearing black shirts than red shirts?

(A) 6 (B) 4

(C) 8 (D) 2

7 In the given table, which bird appears to have been counted twice as many times as the sparrow?

BIRDS			
Parrot	Sparrow	Crow	Pigeon
7	16	8	9

(A) Parrot   (B) Crow   (C) Pigeon   (D) None

8 **Use the line plot:** How many toasters are 11 inches tall?

Height of Toasters

```
          X           X
          X           X                 X
          X           X       X         X
    X     X     X     X       X         X       X       X
  ─────────────────────────────────────────────────────────
    7     8     9     10      11        12      13      14      15
                            Inches
```

(A) 9   (B) 3   (C) 2   (D) 1

4.5   **Graphing and Data**

9   This picture graph shows the number of people who eat each type of ice cream.

Favorite type of Ice-creams

Strawberries	●	●	●
Vanilla	●		
Chocolate	● ● ● ●		

● = 2 People

Noah believes 3 more people eat chocolate ice cream than vanilla ice cream. Do you agree? Explain your reasoning.

_____

10   This picture graph shows the number of miles a butterfly flies each day. From Monday to Wednesday, the butterfly flies 52 miles. Complete the picture graph to show how many miles the butterfly flies on Wednesday

Miles Traveled

Monday	●	●	●	
Tuesday	●	●	●	●
Wednesday				

● = 4 Miles

_____

11 This picture graph shows the number of cakes sold.

Number of cake sold

Monday	● ● ●
Tuesday	● ●
Wednesday	● ● ● ●

● = 3 Cakes

How many cakes were sold altogether? _____.

12 How many more people like broccoli than green beans?

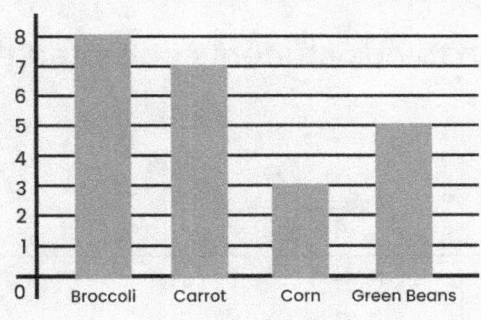

A) 8   B) 5

C) 4   D) 3

13 This picture graph shows the number of books read by 3 students in second grade during the month of May.

Books read

Olivia	● ● ● ●
Liam	● ●
Emma	●

● = 5 Books

How many books did the students read altogether?

4.5 **Graphing and Data**

14 This bar graph displays the number of students who collected each type of item during their summer vacation.

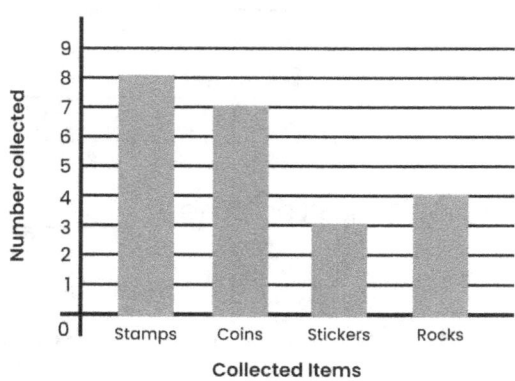

How would you determine which things students collected the most of?

_____

15 Use the data from this table to create a line plot in the space below.

Height of trees (inches)	Number of trees
19	1
14	1
16	1
18	3
12	3
15	4

How many data points are on this line plot?

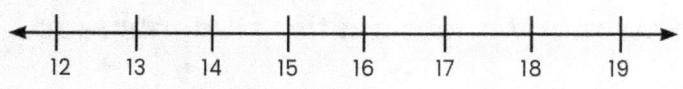

16 Sarah measures the height of a sunflower every week. This table shows her data.

Which line plot represents this data?

Week	Height (cm)
1	18
2	18
3	17
4	20

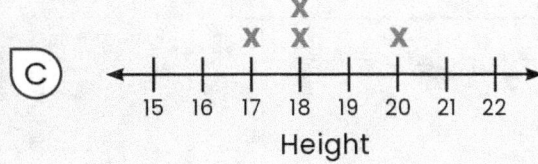

(A)

Weeks

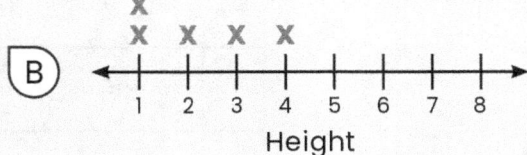

(B)

Height

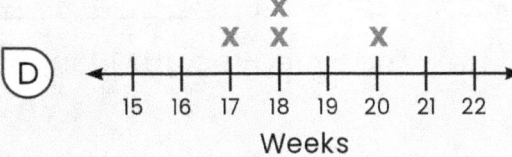

(C)

Height

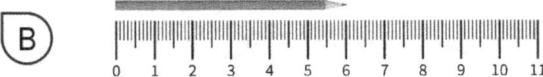

(D)

Weeks

17 Emily uses a ruler to measure the length of these 4 pencils.

(A)

(B)

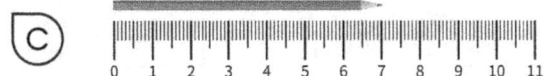

(C)

(D)

Write the length of each pencil in the table

Pencil	A	B	C	D
Pencil (cm)				

4.5 **Graphing and Data**

18 Use the data from this table to create the line plot below.

Length (inches)	Number of leaves
8	✝✝✝✝✝
9				
10				
11			

How many leaves are 10 inches or longer?

_____

19 Daniel collects data on the lengths of different cucumbers at his nearby Walmart.

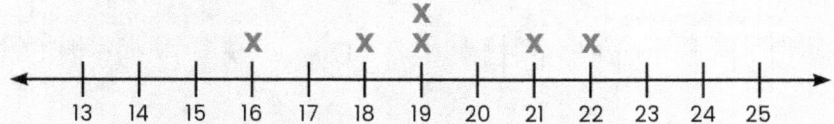

What is the difference between the longest and the shortest cucumbers?

_____ inches.

20 Use the vertical pictograph to answer the question.

Number of cake sold

Tennis Shoes	● ● ● ●
High Heels	●
Sandals	● ●
Boots	● ● ●

● = 2 Persons

How many people chose either boots or high heels?

(A) 8   (B) 6   (C) 4   (D) 2

Next Section: Chapter Review ⟩⟩

4.6   Chapter Review

1 Decide which measurement tool would be the best to measure the length of an object.

Length of a Stick _____.

(A) Ruler   (B) Yardstick   (C) Measuring Tape

2 Eda is measuring how wide the nightstand in his room is. What measurement tool should she use?

_____

3 A Bamboo tree measures 55 centimeters tall. The next week it measures 75 centimetres tall. How many centimeters did the Bamboo plant grow over the week?

(A) 20   (B) 15   (C) 25   (D) 16

4 James and Tom are measuring the height of a photo frame. James says the wall is 6 meters tall. Tom says the wall is 600 centimeters tall. Their mom tells them they are both correct. Why are they both correct?

_____

5 Rachel is 30 inches tall. Her elder brother Bob is 7 inches taller than Rachel. How tall is Bob?

(A) 40 inches (B) 37 inches (C) 50 inches (D) 42 inches

6 A Drumstick is _____ wide.

(A) 12 inches (B) 12 centimeters

(C) 12 feet (D) 12 meters

7 The bat in the picture below is _____ long.

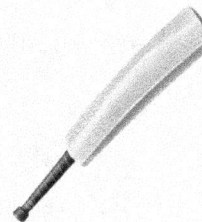

(A) 18 inches (B) 18 centimeters

(C) 12 feet (D) 12 meters

8 What are longer 3 centimetres or 3 inches? Explain your thinking.

_____

4.6   **Chapter Review**

9   Sam says that his house is 6 yards in length. Manuel says that Sam's house is 6 feet. Who is correct? Explain your thinking.

_____

10   What is longer 700 meters or 700 inches? Explain your thinking.

_____

11   Choose which unit of measurement would be best to estimate the height of an object. A Rat _____.

(A) Meters   (B) Feet   (C) Inches   (D) Centimeters

12   Estimate the length, width, or height of the item.
How long do you think a baseball is?

(A) 5 Meters   (B) 5 Feet   (C) 5 Inches   (D) 5 Centimeters

13 Estimate the length, width, or height of the item.
How wide is a pomegranate? _____.

14 Estimate the length, width, or height of the picture in inches or centimeters. Use a ruler to measure the actual length, width, or height of the picture. Find the difference in your estimated length, width, or height of the picture and the actual length, width, or height of the picture.

How tall do you think the watch is? _____ centimeters
What is the actual height of the watch? _____ centimeters

What is the difference between your estimated length of the clock and the actual length of the watch?

_____

15 Ms. Allen is trying to estimate the width of a Chair.
What unit of measurement could Ms. Allen use to estimate the width of a Chair?

_____

16 Draw a picture of a ruler to help solve these subtraction problems with length. With subtraction move to the left (toward smaller numbers on the ruler). 50cm - 17cm = _____cm.

Ⓐ 33 cm   Ⓑ 22 cm   Ⓒ 38 cm   Ⓓ 35 cm

17   65 cm + 12 cm = _____ cm.

    (A) 68 cm   (B) 77 cm   (C) 85 cm   (D) 74 cm

18   Cynthia has 4 boxes stacked on top of each other.
Each box is 6 cm tall. How tall are the 4 boxes stacked together?

    (A) 31   (B) 24   (C) 29   (D) 19

19   Raleigh is buying wire at the hardware store. He is deciding between a wire that is 5 yards long and a foil that is 9 feet long. Both wires are the same price. Which wire should Raleigh buy?

_____

20   Aaron weighs 600 lbs. Timon weighs 727 lbs. How much did Aaron and Timon weigh together?

    (A) 1327   (B) 1463   (C) 1358   (D) 1483

Next Chapter: Time and Money »

CHAPTER 5

TIME AND MONEY

156

FOUNDATIONS OF TELLING TIME

Clocks are used to tell what time it is. There are two types of clocks.

 This is a digital clock. The numbers on a digital clock tell you what time it is. The clock shows that it is 4 o'clock.

This is an analog clock. The hands on an analog clock must be used to tell the time. There are 3 hands on an analog clock. The shortest hand is the hour hand, which shows you what hour it is. The longer hand is the minute hand, which shows you how many minutes it is past the hour.

The skinnier hand is the second hand. It shows how many seconds it is past the minute shown by the minute hand. We will focus on the hour and minute hands. The clock below shows 5:05.

When you are figuring out the hour on an analog clock you will count by 1's. When the hour hand is pointing at the 1 it means it is 1 o'clock. When the hour hand is pointing to the 6 it means it is 6 o'clock. If the hour hand is between two numbers, it means the hour is the first number. Until the hour hand gets all the way to the next number, the hour will still be the first number.

When you are figuring out the minute on an analog clock you will count by 5's. When the minute hand is pointing to the 1 it means it is 5 minutes past the hour. When the minute hand is pointing to the 6 it means it is 30 minutes past the hour. When the minute hand moves to 0, it means it changes to the next hour and the minutes are 0.

5.1   **Foundations of Telling Time**

---

1 Joseph states that the clock shows the minutes are 50. Is he correct? Explain your thinking.

(A) Correct

(B) Incorrect

---

2 What is your dinner time?   (A) A.M.   (B) P.M.

---

3 What hand on an analog clock do you use to determine the hour on an analog clock?

(A) Hour hand   (B) Minute Hand   (C) Second Hand

---

4 Decide if the event happens in the A.M. or P.M. Circle the correct answer. Afternoon recess _____.

(A) 2:00 A.M.   (B) 2:00 P.M.

---

5 James and Jack buy a bottle of orange juice from the store as they are walking to school in the morning. Would this happen at 8:30 A.M. or 8:30 P.M.? Explain your thinking.

(A) 8.30 A.M.   (B) 8.30 P.M.

6 Decide what hour is shown on the clock.

(A) 1

(B) 2

(C) 3

(D) 4

7 What do you skip count by when you are figuring out what minute is shown on an analog clock?

(A) 1's

(B) 10's

(C) 5's

(D) 30's

8 Decide what hour is shown on the clock.

(A) 4'oclock

(B) 5'oclock

(C) 6'oclock

(D) 7'oclock

9 Decide what minute is shown on the clock.

(A) 10

(B) 20

(C) 2

(D) 1

10 Decide what hour is shown on the clock.

(A) 3

(B) 2

(C) 6

(D) 8

5.1   **Foundations of Telling Time**

11   Decide if the event happens in the AM or PM. Circle the correct answer. Eating an evening snack

(A) 5:00 a.m.   (B) 5:00 p.m.

12   Decide what minute is shown on the clock.

(A) 9   (B) 2
(C) 52   (D) 50

13   Decide what minute is shown on the clock.

(A) 0   (B) 60
(C) 12   (D) 1

14   Mia looks at the clock in her kitchen and is trying to figure out what time it is. What hour is shown on the clock below?

(A) 25   (B) 5
(C) 2   (D) 7

15   Kerry looks at the clock in her car, so she knows what time it is. What minute(s) are shown on the clock?

(A) 5   (B) 10
(C) 40   (D) 8

16   What time do you go to school?

(A) AM   (B) PM

17 Mr. Ethan is teaching a lesson about how to tell time on an analog clock that does not have numbers like the one below. Use words and pictures to show how Mr. Ethan might explain how to tell the time using an analog clock that does not have numbers on it.

_____

18 James thinks that the clock below shows that the hour is 7. Is he correct? Explain your thinking.

A Correct   **B** Incorrect

19 What is your breakfast time?   **A** AM   **B** PM

20 What do you skip count by when you are figuring out what hour is shown on an analog clock?

A 1's   **B** 10's   **C** 5's   **D** 30's

Next Section:
Telling Time in Minutes   ≫

TELLING TIME IN MINUTES

When telling time on an analog clock, the hour and minutes hands must be used. The hour hand will tell you what the hour is and the minute hand will tell you what the minute is.

The first step is to figure out what the hour is. When you are figuring out the hour on an analog clock you will count by 1's. If the hour hand is between two numbers, it means the hour is the first number. Until the hour hand gets all the way to the next number, the hour will still be the first number.

The hour hand is pointing to the number 10, which means the hour is 10.

Telling Time in Minutes | **5.2**

1 Emily and Ava start a load of laundry at the time shown on the clock. The loading is done 3 hours later. How long did it take to wash and dry the load of laundry?

_____

2 Draw an analog clock to the time written 6:25.

Hour hand on _____

Minute hand on _____

3 Figure out what time is shown on the clock.

- A) 1:00
- B) 2:00
- C) 3:00
- D) 4:00

4 Figure out what time is shown on the clock.

- A) 5:20
- B) 5:25
- C) 6:30
- D) 6:25

5 Draw the hour and minute hands on the clock to make the correct time 6:30

Hour hand at _____ and minute hand at _____

5.2 **Telling Time in Minutes**

6 Draw the hour and minute hands on the clock to make the correct time 8:55

Hour hand at _____ and minute hand at _____

7 Fill in the clock so they show at the same time.

The hour hand on _____ and the minute hand on _____

8 Fill in the clocks so they show at the same time.

9 Emily states that the clock shows the time 3:05. Is she correct? Explain your thinking.

(A) Correct

(B) Incorrect

10 Jacob tells his teacher that the time on the clock is 4:30. Is Jacob correct? Explain your thinking.

(A) Correct

(B) Incorrect

11 Liam drives his truck to the construction site he is working at. He looks at his watch to see what time it is. The clock below shows what time it was. What time was it?

A) 8:04   B) 9:04   C) 8:20   D) 9:20

12 Mason thinks the clocks show at the same time. Is he correct? Explain your thinking.

13 Harper and Noah are working together on their math project. They are making an analog and a digital clock that both show the time 11:10. What might their clocks look like? Use the analog clock template to help you.

Hour hand on _____ and minute hand on _____

14 Draw an analog clock to the time written. 7:45

Hour hand at _____ and minute hand at _____

5.2 **Telling Time in Minutes**

15 James tells his friend Ava that the clock shows the time 11:00. Is James correct? Explain your thinking.

Ⓐ Correct

Ⓑ Incorrect

16 Draw an analog clock to the time written.
Half past 8

hour hand on _____.
minute hand on _____.

17 Ethan, Emma, and Emily leave the playground at the time on the clock below. They came to the playground 1 hour before that. When did they come to the playground?

_____

18 Draw an analog clock to the time written.
Quarter till 10

hour hand on _____.
minute hand on _____.

19 Draw an analog clock to show the time written. Make sure the numbers are in the correct spaces and are equally spaced.

Quarter past 6

hour hand on _____ and minute hand on _____.

20 Draw an analog clock to show the time written.

Mia leaves a grocery store at the time shown on the clock. She had been in the grocery store for 20 minutes. When did Mia go into the grocery store?

_____

Next Section:
Counting Coins and Bills

COUNTING COINS AND BILLS

Lesson Introduction:

In this lesson, we will learn how to count coins and dollar bills together! When we count coins and bills, we always need to keep these two steps in mind.

1. Count the bills first.

2. Then, count the coins starting with larger values.

Let's look at this example.

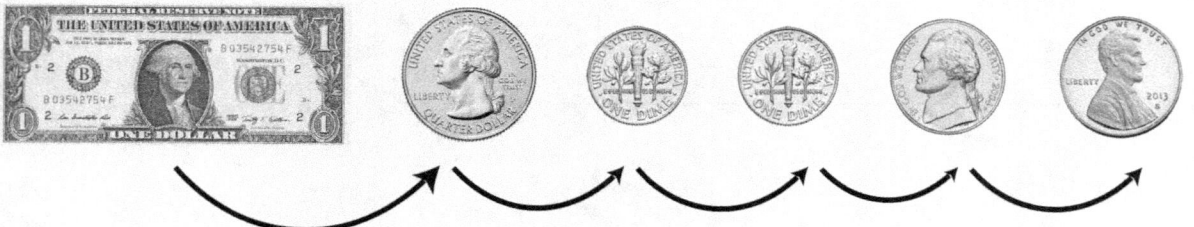

We have 1 dollar bill, 1 quarter, 2 dimes, 1 nickel, and 1 penny. First, we start with the dollar bill, $1.00. Then count the coins starting with larger values and count on, 1.25...1.35...1.45...1.50...1.51. So the total value of these coins is $1.51.

1 Briton has 2 one-dollar billsand 9 quarters. Brady has 4 one-dollar bills. Who has more money, Briton or Brady? Show your work.

Ⓐ Briton Ⓑ Brady

2 An orange juice costs $2.35. Sam has 6 quarters. Does he have enough money to buy orange juice?

Ⓐ Yes Ⓑ No

3 A pencil costs 55¢. Kenny paid for it with 3 quarters. How much change will he get?

Ⓐ 40 cents Ⓑ 30 cents Ⓒ 20 cents Ⓓ 10 cents

4 Collin has 4 one-dollar bills, 5 pennies, and 2 dimes. How much money does he have in total?

Ⓐ $4.75 Ⓑ $4.30 Ⓒ $4.20 Ⓓ $4.25

5 Jack went to the bookstore to buy his favorite chapter book. He spent 1 quarter, 3 pennies, and 1 dime. How much money did he spend on the book?

Ⓐ 35 cents Ⓑ 38 cents Ⓒ 30 cents Ⓓ 40 cents

5.3   **Counting Coins and Bills**

6   Ivy wants to buy a notebook. One notebook cost $1.50. She has a dollar bill, 2 quarters, and 2 nickels. Does she have enough money to buy one notebook?

     (A) Yes   (B) No

7   Zelda has 2 quarters, 2 dimes, and 2 pennies. Does she have enough money to buy stickers that cost 80¢?

     (A) Yes   (B) No

8   Emily found a dollar bill, 5 nickels and 3 quarters in a locker. How much money did she find altogether?

     (A) $1.00   (B) $2.00   (C) $1.75   (D) $2.54

9   Mrs. Saul went to the store to buy pencils. A pencil cost 30¢. She has 6 nickels and 10 pennies. Does she have enough money to buy one pencil?

     (A) Yes   (B) No

10   Justin went to the store to buy a donut. He spent 2 one-dollar bills, 3 dimes, 4 pennies, and 2 nickels. How much money did he spend on the donut?

     (A) $2.90   (B) $2.60   (C) $2.45   (D) $2.44

11 Parker wants to buy a new Pokémon card. It costs 90¢. He has 3 quarters and 3 nickels. Does he have enough money to buy the Pokémon card?

A) Yes   B) No

12 Ivy has 4 dimes and 3 nickels. Liliya has 4 quarters and 2 dimes. Which skip-counting strategy can be used to count the values of these coins?

A) 25, 50, 75, 100, 110, 120, 130, 140, 150, 160, 165, 170, 175

B) 25, 50, 60, 70, 80, 90, 100, 110, 115, 120, 125

C) 1, 2, 3, 4, 5, 6, 7, 8, 9, 10, 11

D) 25, 50, 55, 60, 65, 70, 75, 80, 85, 90, 95

13 Harston went to the beach. She spent 3 one-dollar bills, 3 quarters, 3 nickels, and 3 dimes for the entry ticket. How much money did she spend on the entry ticket?

A) $4.00   B) $4.10   C) $4.20   D) $4.30

14 Asher wants to buy a water gun that costs $1.70.
He has 1 one-dollar bill, 2 quarters, and 10 pennies. Does he have enough money to buy the water gun?

A) Yes   B) No

5.3 Counting Coins and Bills

15 How much money is shown by the coins?

A) 26¢   B) 18¢   C) 16¢   D) 20¢

16 How much money is shown by the coins?

A) 22¢   B) 32¢   C) 23¢   D) 30¢

17 Mia has 4 quarters, 4 dimes, and 3 nickels in her piggy bank. How much does she have in her piggy bank?

A) $1.55   B) $1.75

C) $1.45   D) $1.30

18 Work out the correct total for these coins and bills.

two-dollar bills + 3 pennies + 2 quarters + 5 nickels = $ _____.

19 A cookie costs 10¢ each. A chocolate cost 15¢ each. Victor has 2 quarters, 2 dimes, and 2 pennies. Does he have enough money to buy two cookies and two chocolates?

(A) Yes   (B) No

20 How much money is shown by the coins and bills?

(A) $4.75   (B) $4.00   (C) $4.50   (D) $4.73

Next Section:
Word Problems with Money

173

WORD PROBLEMS WITH MONEY

Lesson Introduction:

Now that we know how to count coins and bills, we can solve many kinds of real-life word problems! Let's look at some word problems and use what we have learned so far.

Emma and her mom went to the grocery store to buy ingredients for chocolate brownies. Look at the pictures below and answer the questions.

First, let's examine the chart. The picture shows what they bought in the grocery store. The coins and bills show how much each item is.

How much is the milk?

There are 2 one-dollar bills, 3 dimes, and 1 penny. Let's add them up.

$2.00 + $0.30 + $0.01 = $2.31. So, the milk costs $2.31.

1   Saul has 8 dimes and 9 nickels. Seth has 2 more dimes and 4 fewer nickels than Saul. How much money do Saul and Seth have together?

Saul and Seth _____

2   This is the school lunch menu.

Lunch Menu						
Item	Milk	Chicken Nuggets	Salad	Juice	Fries	Water
Cost	50¢	$2.10	$1.55	$1.00	55¢	40¢

Mia has 2 one-dollar bills, 4 quarters, 7 dimes, and 5 nickels. Which menu items is she able to buy with the least amount of money left over?

(A) Chicken Nuggets, Water, and Salad   (C) Milk and Water

(B) Chicken Nuggets and Salad   (D) Salad, Juice, and Fries

3   Liam has 6 one-dollar and 10 dimes. Noah has 5 one-dollar bills and 10 quarters. Who has more money, Liam or Noah?

_____

5.4   **Word Problems with Money**

4   Ruby puts 5 one-dollar bills and 4 pennies in her bank. She now has $10.90 in the bank. How much money did Ruby start with?

A) $5.90   B) $5.60   C) $5.45   D) $5.86

5   Briar has 55 cents. Greer has 20 cents more than Briar. Joe has 25 cents more than Greer. How much money do they have altogether?

A) $2.20   B) $2.30   C) $1.00   D) $2.00

6   Henry has 4 quarters, 4 dimes, 6 nickels, and 6 pennies. He spends half of his money on candy. How much money does Henry have left?

_____

7   Kim has 6 quarters, 4 dimes, 2 nickels, and 12 pennies. Ava has 8 quarters, 6 dimes, 1 nickel, and 10 pennies. How could you determine who has more money? Explain your reasoning.

_____

8 Ryan has a one-dollar bill. He wants to give $0.25 to his friends. How can Ryan exchange his one-dollar bill for other coins so he can give money to his friend? Explain your reasoning.

_____

How much money would Ryan have left?

_____

9 Emily went to the water park on Sunday. Look at the prices below and answer the questions.

 $1.80    $2.60 $2.90    $2.10

Emily bought ice cream. She gave the clerk 1 one-dollar bill, 4 quarters, 2 dimes, and 4 nickels. How much change did she get back?

(A) $0.6   (B) $0.5   (C) $0.45   (D) $0.36

10 Adam wants to buy a pen that costs $4.00. He has 1 one-dollar bill, 20 dimes, 10 pennies. Does he have enough money to buy the pen?

(A) Yes   (B) No

5.4 Word Problems with Money

11 Rita has $2.65 in her pocket. One pencil cost $1.60.
How many pencils can she buy? _____

12 Zoey has quarters that are worth $3.00. If she puts one quarter in the candy machine, she will get one candy. With her $3.00, how many candies can she get from the candy machine?

_____

13 Amir has 1 one-dollar bill, 8 quarters, and 2 nickels. Does he have enough money to buy a bar of soap that costs $3.00?

Ⓐ Yes   Ⓑ No

14 Rhett bought a pack of fireworks that cost $4.78. He gave the clerk 5 one-dollar bills and 4 dimes.
How much change did he get back? _____

15 Oliver has 5 one-dollar bills. Oliver bought a pair of sunglasses that costs $4.98.
How much money does he have left? _____

16 Mr. Aden bought a pack of pencils that cost $5.89. He gave the clerk 6 one-dollar bills.
How much change will he get? _____

17 Rhoda has 4 one-dollar bills, 3 dimes, and 5 nickels. Ava has 4 one-dollar bills and 8 nickels.
Who has more money, Rhoda or Ava?

Ⓐ Rhoda   Ⓑ Ava

18 David and Peter made a juice stand to earn money so they could buy a brand-new basketball. Look at the chart and answer the questions.

Juices	Cost
Orange Juice	$0.46
Peach Juice	$0.50
Grape Juice	$0.39

A customer wants to buy orange juice and peach juice. How much would both juices cost?

Ⓐ $0.86   Ⓑ $0.96

Ⓒ $0.80   Ⓓ $0.90

5.4   **Word Problems with Money**

19 Ruby and her mom went to the grocery store. Look at the prices below and answer the question.

 $2.80    $2.05 $2.30 $2.35

Ruby brought her piggy bank with her. She has 8 quarters and 4 dimes. How much change does she get if she buys one avocado?

(A) $0.08   (B) $0.05   (C) $0.06   (D) $0.10

20 Elijah is selling his old toys in a yard sale. Look at the prices below and answer the question.

 $3    $2.45    $2.00

Noah wants to buy the car. He has 8 quarter and 10 dimes. How much money does he have left if he buys one car?

(A) $0   (B) $1.00   (C) $2.00   (D) $0.25

Next Section: Chapter Review ≫

1 Vinci has $2.75. He then receives 5 dimes and 4 pennies from his sister. Vinci's brother gives her twice as much money as his sister gave him. How much money does Vinci have now?

(A) $2.37   (B) $3.37   (C) $4.37   (D) $5.37

2 Which digital clock matches the time shown on this analog clock?

(A)
(B)
(C)
(D)

3 Britta uses this strategy to determine the time shown on the clock.

"First, I know that the hour hand is between 11 and 12, which means it is after 11 O'Clock. Next, I count by five, 10 times. 5, 10, 15, 20, 25, 30, 35, 40, 45, 50. The time showing on the clock is 11:50."

Do you agree with Britta? Explain your reasoning.

5.5   **Chapter Review**

4   This clock shows when school ends.

After school, Emma spends 10 minutes walking home. Where would the hour and minute hands be on the clock when Emma arrives home?

(A)   The hour hand is on the 4, and the minute hand is on the 12.

(B)   The hour hand is on the 3, and the minute hand is on the 12.

(C)   The hour hand is between the 3 and 4, and the minute hand is on the 8.

(D)   The hour hand is on the 5, and the minute hand is on the 12.

5   Ruth is feeding her dog and cat. This clock shows the time Ruth starts feeding both animals.

Ruth feeds her dog first. The dog takes 45 minutes to eat his food. Ruth's cat takes a few 15 minutes less than the dog.
What time does Ruth's cat finish eating? Explain your reasoning.

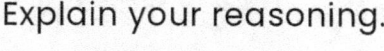

6 Jenny has 4 quarters and 2 nickels. Vinci has 4 dimes, 2 nickels, and 10 pennies. Ava has 1 dollar and 5 dimes. Harston has 8 quarters, 4 dimes, and 8 pennies.

Which list shows a comparison of the amount of money each one has, in order from greatest to least?

(A) Jenny, Vinci, Ava, Harston

(B) Jenny, Vinci, Harston, Ava

(C) Harston, Vinci, Jenny, Ava

(D) Harston, Ava, Jenny, Vinci

7 On Monday, Marson put $2.10 in his bank. He put the same amount of money in his bank on Tuesday, Wednesday, and Thursday. How much money did Marson put in the bank?

_____

8 The clock shows the time music class starts.

The music class is 30 minutes long. What time does the music class end?

(A) 3:30   (B) 3:45   (C) 4:00   (D) 3:40

5.5 Chapter Review

9 Peter is riding the bus from his house to his grandfather's house. This clock shows the time he arrives.

The bus ride is 15 minutes long. Where would the hour and minute hands be on a clock at the time Peter leaves his house?

_____

10 Rome rides her bike for 30 minutes. This clock shows the time she stops riding her bike.

What time did Rome start riding her bike?

(A) 2:10   (B) 2:00   (C) 2:20   (D) 2:30

11 This clock shows the time Briar leaves her school on a bus.

The bus ride home is a few 15 minutes long. The walk from the bus stop to Briar's house is a few 10 minutes. What time does Briar arrive home?

(A) 5:00   (B) 5:10   (C) 4:55   (D) 5:20

12 Kerry takes 25 minutes to bake one pan of muffins. She is baking 2 pans of muffins, and she starts baking at 9:10 a.m. Draw the time Kerry finishes baking.

13 Joel leaves his friend's house at 3:55 pm. It takes him 10 minutes
to walk home. Draw the time when Joel arrives home.

14 This clock shows the time Max arrives at his friend's house.

Thirty-five minutes later, he returns home. When he arrives home, he takes a few 45 minutes to eat dinner. What time does Max finish dinner?

15 Travis watches TV for 1 hour. This clock shows the time he starts watching TV.

What time does Travis stop watching TV?

A) 4:00   B) 4:05   C) 4:10   D) 4:20

5.5 **Chapter Review**

16 Parker works on homework for 10 minutes. When he finishes, it is half past nine. Draw the time Parker finishes his homework on the clock.

17 How many minutes have passed since 7:00? Explain your reasoning.

_____

18 $0.22 is the money Zelda has saved. Zelda's father gives her 44 more cents. How much money does Zelda have now?

(A) $0.66   (B) $0.48   (C) $0.65   (D) $0.55

19 Tara thinks the clocks below show the same time. Is she correct? Explain your thinking.

(A) Correct   (B) Incorrect

20 Draw the hour and minute hands on the clock. 7:15.

Next Chapter: Geometry

CHAPTER 6

GEOMETRY

ATTRIBUTES OF BASIC SHAPES

In this lesson, we are going to look at the attributes of shapes. Any 2-dimensional shape formed with straight lines is called a polygon. Let's look at each polygon and find out how many corners and sides they have!

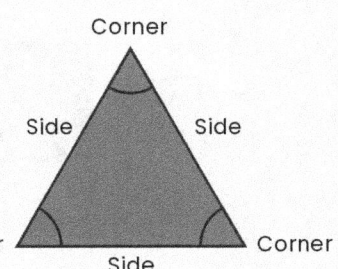

This is a triangle. A triangle has 3 corners (angles) and 3 sides.

A quadrilateral has 4 corners (angles) and 4 sides. A Square, Rectangle, Rhombus, and Trapezoid are also quadrilaterals.

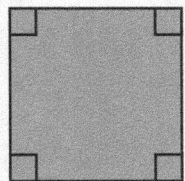

Square

4 Equal sides
all angles are 90°

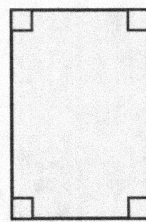

Rectangle

Equal opposite sides
all angles are 90°

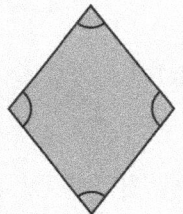

Rhombus

4 Equal sides and opposite
sides are parallel

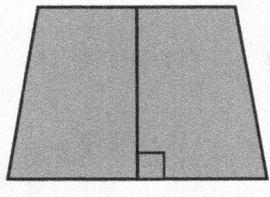

Trapezoid

2 sides are parallel

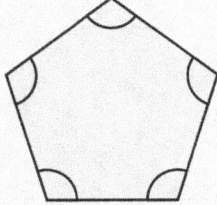

This is a pentagon.

A pentagon has 5 corners
(angles) and 5 sides.

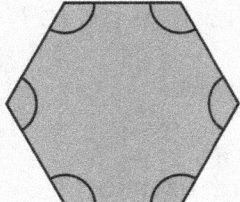

This is a hexagon.

A hexagon has 6 corners
(angles) and 6 sides.

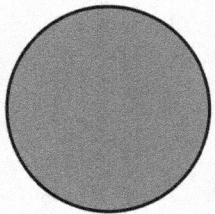

This is a circle.

A Circle has 0 corners
(angles) and 0 sides.

6.1   **Attributes of Basic Shapes**

1   Choose a shape that is not a quadrilateral.

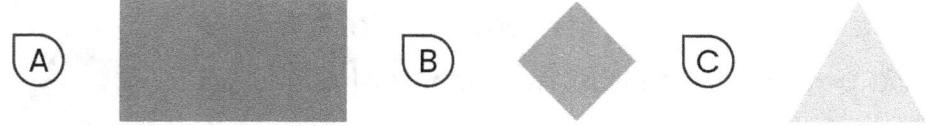

2   Which shape is a pentagon?

3   Choose the trapezoid.

4   How many sides does a triangle have? _____.

5   How many corners does a hexagon have? _____.

6   How many corners does a quadrilateral have? _____.

Attributes of Basic Shapes **6.1**

7 How many corners does a circle have? _____

8 How many circles are there?_____

9 How many hexagons are there? _____

10 A Rhombus has _____ corners and _____ sides.

11 Say whether it is true or false: (A) True   (B) False
A circle has 3 corners and 4 sides.

12 Sam drew a shape with 6 sides and 6 corners.
What shape did he draw? _____

6.1   **Attributes of Basic Shapes**

13 Say whether it is true or false:
A square has 4 corners and 4 sides

(A) True   (B) False

14 I am a shape that has 5 sides. What am I? _____

15 Mr. James asked his students to draw a circle. Jenny drew a shape with 3 sides and 3 corners. Robert drew a shape with 0 sides and 0 corners. Who is correct, Jenny or Robert? Explain why.

(A) Robert   (B) Jenny

16 Name the shape that has 4 sides and 4 corners. _____

17 How many sides does the following shape have?

18 Mike drew a shape with 6 sides and 6 corners.
What shape did he draw?_____

19 Say whether it is true or false:

Mike drew a shape with 4 corners and 4 sides. He drew a rectangle.

(A) True   (B) False

20 I am a shape that has 3 sides.

What am I? _____.

Next Section:
Attributes of Complex Shapes ≫

ATTRIBUTES OF COMPLEX SHAPES

In this lesson, we are going to take a look at complex shapes. We have two different kinds of polygons, regular polygons and irregular polygons.

Let's take a look at regular polygons. A regular polygon has all sides equal and all angles equal. Square, triangle, pentagon, and hexagon are examples of regular polygons because all of their sides and angles are congruent (same).

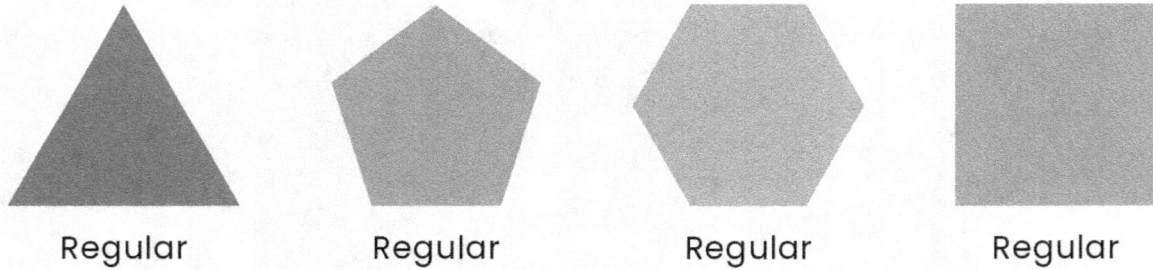

Regular   Regular   Regular   Regular

These are irregular polygons. An irregular polygon does not have all sides equal and all angles equal. These are examples of irregular polygons.

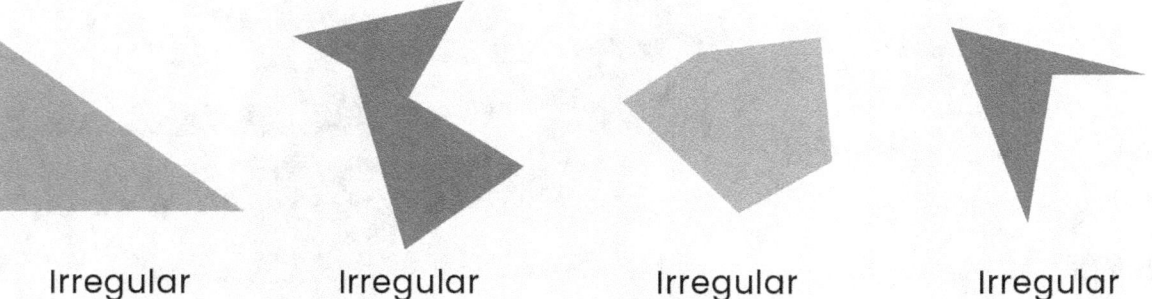

Irregular   Irregular   Irregular   Irregular

1 Which one is an irregular triangle and why?

2 Which one is a regular square and why?

3 Count the sides and corners

_____ sides and _____ corners

4 There are 2 squares and 2 rectangles.
How many corners are there in total? _____ corners.

5 There are 3 pentagons and 2 hexagons.
How many corners are there in total? _____ corners.

6.2   Attributes of Complex Shapes

6   I am an irregular polygon that has 4 sides and 4 corners.
What am I?_____.

7   Mike drew a shape that has 5 sides that are different in length.
What shape did he draw? _____.

8   How is an irregular triangle different from a regular triangle?
Explain.

_____

9   The only regular quadrilateral is a square. True or False?

(A) True   (B) False

10   How is an irregular square different from a regular square?

_____

11 Jerry drew an irregular pentagon on his paper. How many sides and corners does it have?

Sides = _____   Corners = _____

12 An irregular polygon has congruent sides and angles. True or False?

(A) True   (B) False

13 Ms. Bendy asked her students to draw an irregular triangle. Tim drew picture A, and Mac drew picture B. Who drew the correct irregular triangle?

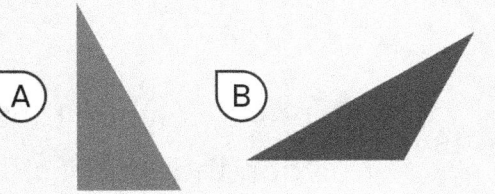

14 Explain:
A regular square and an irregular square are similar because _____. They are different because_____.

15 Identify the type of shape below:
It has _____ sides
and _____ corners. What shape is it?

6.2 Attributes of Complex Shapes

16 Draw lines to complete the shape.
Draw lines to make an irregular triangle.

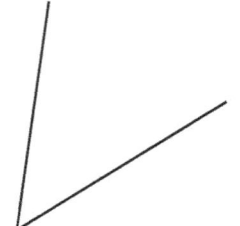

17 Identify the type of shape below.
It is _____.

18 There are 3 triangles and 2 circles.
How many sides are there in total? _____ Sides.

19 Sid has a polygon that has 3 sides and 3 corners. Becky has a polygon that has 4 sides and 4 corners. Who has a square?

A) Sid   B) Becky

20 Jim drew a shape that has 6 sides that are different in length.
What shape did he draw? _____

Next Section:
Recognize and Draw Shapes

RECOGNIZE AND DRAW SHAPES

A 2D shape is a flat plane figure or a shape with two dimensions: Length and width.

Vertices: Vertices are the points where two or more line segments or edges meet.

Faces: A face is a flat surface that forms part of the boundary of a solid object.

Examples of 2D shapes are a Circle, Rectangle, Triangle, Square etc.

The properties of basic figures are as mentioned below.

Rectangle – A rectangle is a 2D shape with four vertices and four sides.

Square – A square is a 2D shape with four vertices and 4 sides with all the sides equal.

Triangle – A triangle is a 2D shape with 3 vertices and sides.

A 3D shape is a solid figure or an object with three dimensions which are length, width and height.

Examples of 3D shapes:

Cube, Cuboid, Sphere, Cone, Cylinder etc.

Example: Jerry has 4 cones. Jack has 4 cylinders. Who has less faces?

Solution:

Jerry has less faces.

4 cones have 4×1 = 4 faces. 4 cylinders have 4×3 = 12 faces.

6.3 **Recognize and Draw Shapes**

1 Tyler has 6 cubes. Eli has 4 rectangular prisms. Who has fewer vertices?

(A) Tyler   (B) Eli

2 Levi has triangles. Evan has triangular prisms. What do those shapes have in common?

(A) Triangle   (B) Rectangle   (C) Square   (D) Prism

3 Julian has 4 cones. Aaron has 4 cylinders. Who has fewer faces?

(A) Julian   (B) Aaron

4 Emma has a square. Ava has a sphere. Who has a shape that has sides?

(A) Emma   (B) Ava

5 Noah has 3 triangular prisms and 3 cubes. How many faces does he have altogether?

(A) 23   (B) 26   (C) 30   (D) 33

6 Peyton drew a cone and said a cone has only 3 faces. Explain why she is wrong.

_____

7 Jose has a 3D shape that has 6 faces. He said he has a cube. Is he correct? Explain your answer.

(A) Yes   (B) No

8 What shape is the die?

_____

9 Is the cone a 2D or 3D shape?

(A) 2D   (B) 3D

10 Is the arrow a 2D or 3D shape?

(A) 2D   (B) 3D

6.3 **Recognize and Draw Shapes**

11 Fill in the blanks with the correct numbers.
Cylinder
Number of vertices: _____

12 Fill in the blanks with the correct numbers.
Rectangular prism
Number of edges: _____

13 I am a shape that has no face. What am I?

(A) Square (B) Sphere

(C) Rectangular prism (D) Cylinder

14 Peter brought a tomato can to school.
What shape is the tomato can?

(A) Cone (B) Square

(C) Circle (D) Cylinder

15 Austin has 4 cubes.
How many vertices does he have altogether?

(A) 24 (B) 30 (C) 32 (D) 48

16 Lucy has 3 cylinders.
How many faces does she have altogether?

(A) 6   (B) 9   (C) 8   (D) 12

17 Kerry has 2 rectangular prisms, and Oliver has 2 square pyramids.
How many faces do they have altogether?

(A) 22   (B) 18   (C) 16   (D) 20

18 Blake has a shape that has 5 sides and 5 corners. Jace has a shape
that has 6 faces, 12 edges and 8 vertices. Which one has a 3D shape?

(A) Blake   (B) Jace

19 What do a square pyramid and a cube have in common?

(A) Triangular faces   (B) Square faces   (C) Rectangular faces

20 Parker has 3 rectangular prisms.
Cooper has 4 triangular prisms. Who has more edges?

(A) Parker   (B) Cooper

Next Section: Chapter Review »

6.4   Chapter Review

1   How many sides does this shape have?

_____

2   How many vertices does this shape have?

_____

3   Kim says a pentagon has more vertices than a hexagon. Is this true? Explain why or why not.

_____

4   **Draw a shape matching this description:**
The shape has 4 sides.

_____

5   **Draw a shape matching this description:**
The shape has two sides with different lengths.

6 Which response describes quadrilaterals?

(A) A quadrilateral has fewer sides than a pentagon.

(B) A quadrilateral has only 3 edges.

(C) A quadrilateral has 6 vertices.

(D) A quadrilateral has more sides than a hexagon.

7 Tom drew a shape with 0 sides and 0 corners.
What shape did he draw? _____.

8 How many sides does this shape have?

_____

9 How many sides does this shape have?

_____

6.4 Chapter Review

10 I am a shape that has 6 sides. What am I? _____.

11 Say whether it is true or false:
A rhombus has 4 corners and 4 sides. Ⓐ True   Ⓑ False

12 Mike drew a shape with 3 sides and 3 corners.
What shape did he draw? _____

13 How many corners does a rectangle have? _____

14 How many vertices does a circle have? _____

15 Draw an irregular pentagon

16 Draw a cube

17 There are 3 rectangles and 2 hexagons. How many corners are there in total? _____ corners.

6.4 Chapter Review

18 I am an irregular polygon that has 5 sides and 5 corners.
What am I? _____.

19 An irregular polygon and a regular polygon have equal sides and angles. True or False?

(A) True   (B) False

20 The shapes below have _____ sides
and _____ corners.

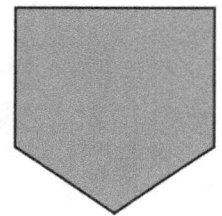

Next Chapter: Fractions

CHAPTER 7

FRACTIONS

FRACTIONS IN HALVES, THIRDS, AND FOURTHS

A fraction is a part of a whole.

Let's take a look at this circle. This is a whole.

Let's split the circle into 2 equal parts.

Now we have two halves.

A half is $\frac{1}{2}$ of the whole.

$\frac{1}{2} + \frac{1}{2} = 1$

2 halves = 1 whole

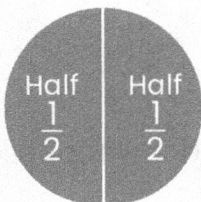

Let's split the circle into 3 equal parts this time.

Now we have thirds.

A third is $\frac{1}{3}$ of the whole.

$\frac{1}{3}$ is 1 out of 3 equal parts.

$\frac{1}{3} + \frac{1}{3} + \frac{1}{3} = 1$

3 thirds = 1 whole

Now let's split the circle into 4 equal parts this time.

Now we have fourths.

A fourth is $\frac{1}{4}$ of the whole.

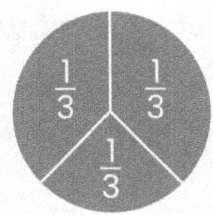

$\frac{1}{4}$ is 1 out of 4 equal parts.

$\frac{1}{4} + \frac{1}{4} + \frac{1}{4} + \frac{1}{4} = 1$

4 fourths = 1 whole.

7.1 **Fractions in Halves, Thirds, and Fourths**

1 Select the picture that shows halves

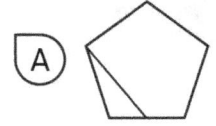 A  B  C  D

2 Choose the fraction that is shown in the picture

 A $\frac{2}{1}$ B $\frac{2}{2}$ C $\frac{1}{2}$ D $\frac{1}{3}$

3 Select the picture that shows thirds

 A 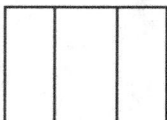 B  C  D

4 The given picture is divided into _____.

5 Select the picture that shows fourths

A 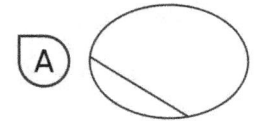   B 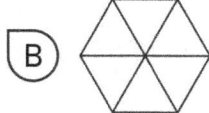   C 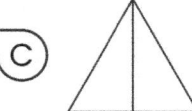   D

6 How many parts are shaded?

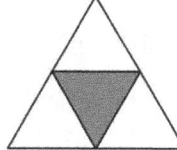

A) One-half   B) One-third

C) One-fourth   D) Whole

7 Choose $\frac{1}{4}$ of the rectangle shaded

A 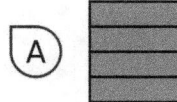   B 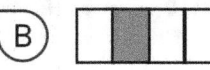  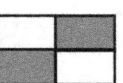   C   D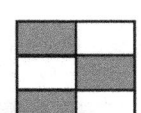

8 How is this shape divided?

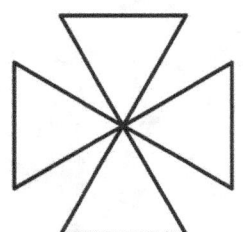 _____

7.1   Fractions in Halves, Thirds, and Fourths

9   How many equal parts are in the given shape?

_____

10   State Yes or No. Do these shapes represent the same fraction?

_____

11   State Yes or No. Do they both represent the same fraction?

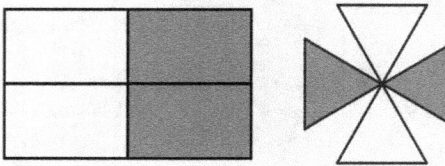

_____

12   What fraction of the fruits below are watermelons?

_____

13 What fraction of the pizza is remaining?

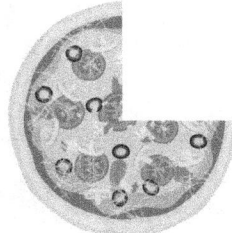

_____

14 What fraction of tomatoes are circled?

_____

15 What fraction of tomatoes are not circled?

_____

16 Matthew gave $\frac{1}{4}$ of pie to his brother Alan.
How much pie does Matthew have left?

_____

7.1   **Fractions in Halves, Thirds, and Fourths**

17   Maria gave $\frac{2}{4}$ of her cake to her mom and $\frac{1}{4}$ of her cake to her dad. How much cake does she have left?

_____

18   Partition the trapezoid into halves.

19   Partition the triangle into thirds.

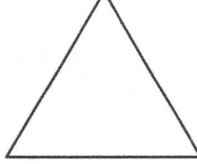

20   How many equal shares does this circle have?

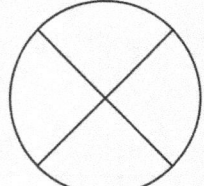 _____

Next Section: Partitioning Circles and Rectangles

PARTITIONING CIRCLES AND RECTANGLES

Partitioning means to split something into different pieces. Shapes can be split into equal sized pieces or different sized pieces.

Look at the rectangles below. All of them are partitioned into 4 pieces. Which rectangles are partitioned into equal sized pieces?

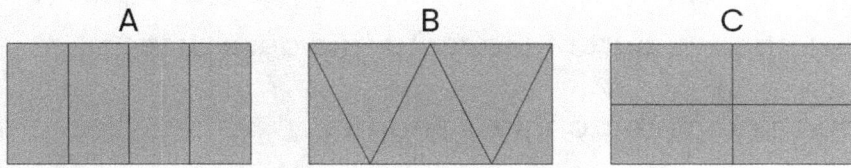

Shape A and C are partitioned into 4 equal sized pieces.

When a shape is partitioned into 4 equal pieces, each piece is called a fourth.

We can draw multiple ways to partition circles and rectangles into halves, thirds, and fourths.

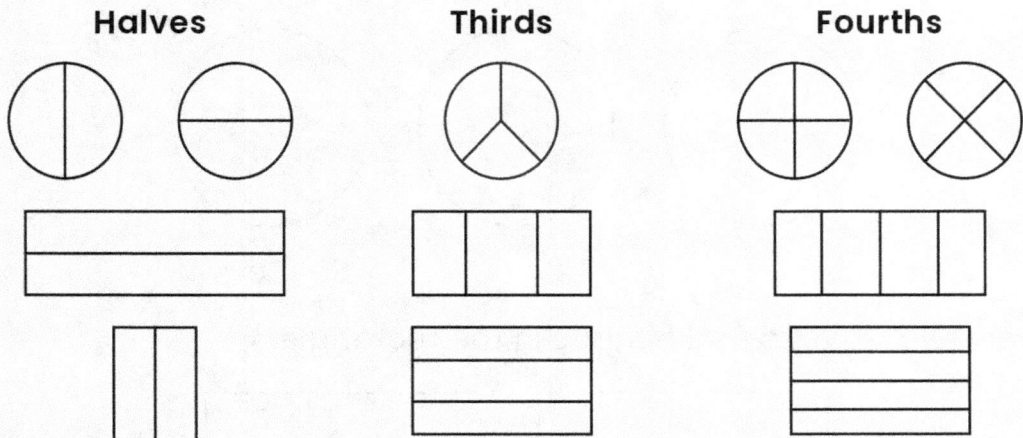

7.2   **Partitioning Circles and Rectangles**

1   Which name describes how the circle is partitioned?

A) Halves   B) Thirds

C) Fourths   D) Whole

2   How is the shaded part of the rectangle described?

A) A fourth of the rectangle is shaded.

B) A third of the rectangle is shaded.

C) Half of the rectangle is shaded.

D) The whole rectangle is shaded.

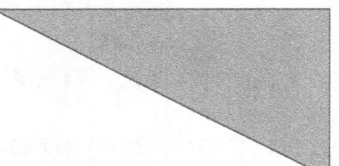

3   Show three ways to make halves in the circle.

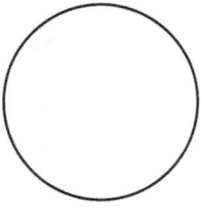 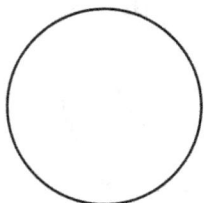 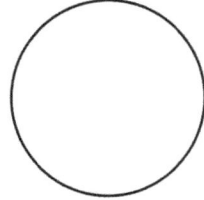

4   Show two ways to make thirds in the rectangle.

 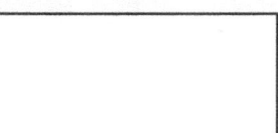

5 Show two ways to make fourths in the circle.

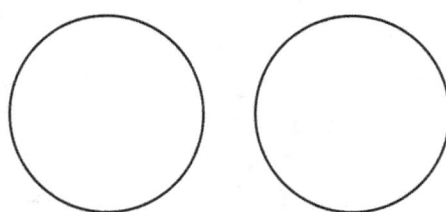

6 Dalton cut an apple into four equal parts. He gave one part to his friend Jack and another part to his friend Ian.
What fraction of apple did they get together?

A) One-fourth   B) Two-fourths

C) One-third   D) Two-thirds

7 Sam cut the cupcake into four equal parts and ate one part. What fraction of cupcake did he left?

A) Whole   B) Two parts

C) Three parts   D) Four parts

8 Select the circle that is partitioned into two equal parts.

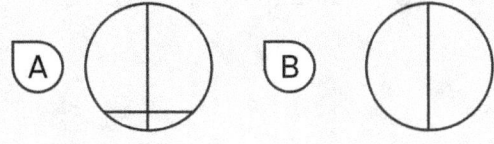

A   B

C   D

7.2 Partitioning Circles and Rectangles

9 Select which rectangle is partitioned into two equal parts and write the fraction.

  _____

10 Atlas wants to cut the pizza into three equal pieces. Choose how he can cut the pizza into three equal pieces.

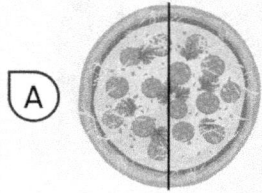 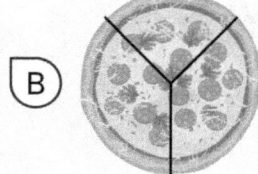 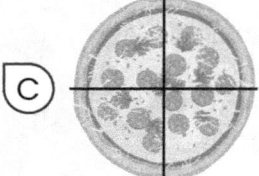

11 Which rectangle is partitioned into four equal parts and has two-fourths shaded?

Ⓐ 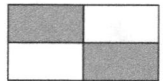 Ⓑ 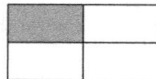 Ⓒ 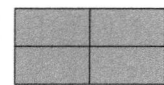 Ⓓ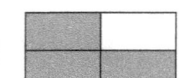

12 **True or False:** The circle is partitioned into four equal parts and two-fourths are shaded.

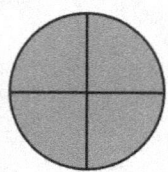

Ⓐ True   Ⓑ False

13 **True or False:** The rectangle is partitioned into four equal parts and three-fourths are shaded.

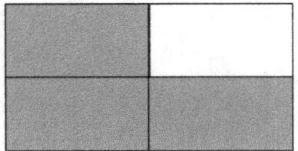

(A) True

(B) False

14 Partition the rectangle into six equal parts.

15 **True or False:** The circle is partitioned into two equal parts, and one half is shaded.

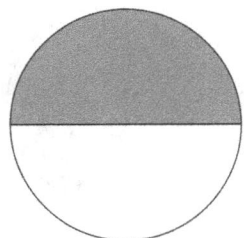

16 Select the rectangle that has seven parts.

(A)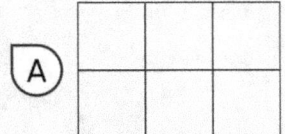

(B)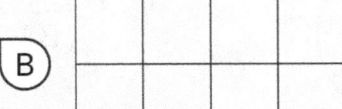

(C)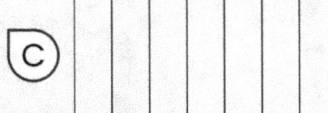

(D)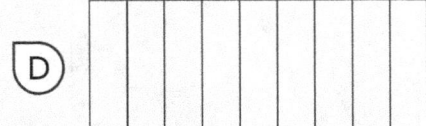

7.2 **Partitioning Circles and Rectangles**

17 Select the rectangle that has five shaded parts.

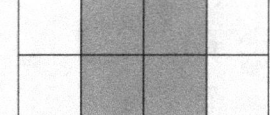 A 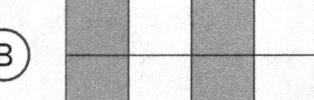 B

 C 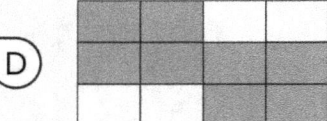 D

18 Select the circle that has three shaded parts.

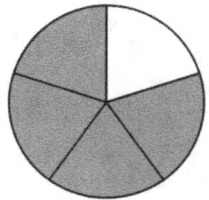 A 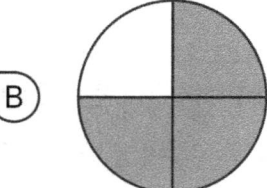 B

19 Select the circle that has eight parts.

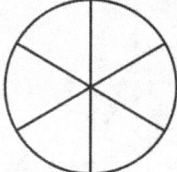 A  B

 C  D

20 Shade three-fourths of the circle.

Next Section: Wholes »

WHOLES

What does a whole mean? What is the difference between $\frac{1}{4}$ and $\frac{4}{4}$

Aaron bought 3 apples. He wants to use one apple to feed his 4 hamsters.

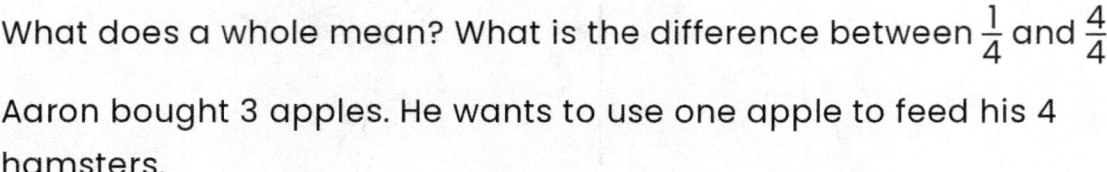

What fraction can we use to show the number of apples?

We have 3 apples, so we have 3 wholes. Any whole number can be written as a fraction by putting the whole number in the numerator (top) and 1 in the denominator (bottom).

So, the answer is $\frac{3}{1}$

What fraction can we use to show the apples he used to feed the hamsters?

This time we are looking at only one apple because he used only one apple to feed his hamsters. He needs to divide the apple into 4 equal pieces to feed his 4 hamsters.

WHOLES

Aaron used 4 out of the 4 parts of the apple.

So, the answer is $\frac{4}{4}$

It is also the same as saying he used the whole apple.

When a fraction has the same numerator (top) and denominator (bottom), it means the same as 1. Even if the fraction is $\frac{100}{100}$.

It still means 1.

7.3   **Wholes**

1   Franklin has 7 toy cars.

(A) $\frac{7}{1}$ (B) $\frac{7}{7}$ (C) $\frac{1}{7}$ (D) $\frac{2}{7}$

2   Ronald cut a watermelon into 12 pieces.

(A) $\frac{1}{12}$ (B) $\frac{6}{12}$ (C) $\frac{12}{1}$ (D) $\frac{12}{12}$

3   Draw lines in a circle to show $\frac{6}{6}$

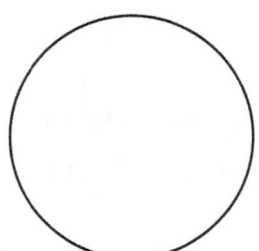

4   Find the value of $\frac{5}{5}$

(A) 5   (B) 1   (C) 3   (D) 4

5   Find the value of $\frac{9}{1}$

(A) 1   (B) 6   (C) 9   (D) 10

6 Which number line represents $\frac{8}{1}$

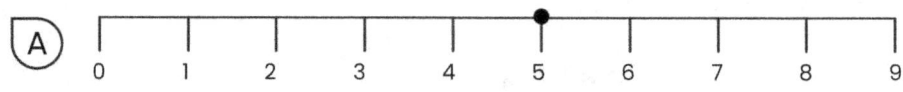

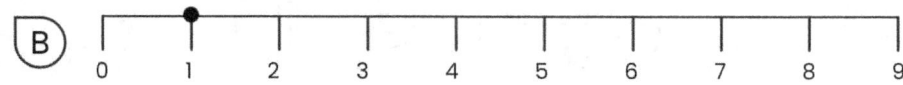

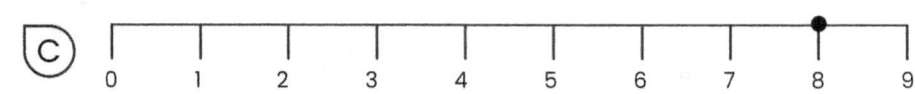

7 Select the picture that shows $\frac{3}{3}$

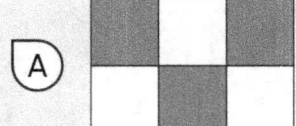

8 Select the picture that shows $\frac{1}{1}$

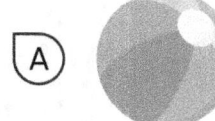

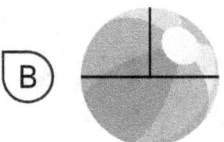

9 Select the picture that shows $\frac{4}{4}$

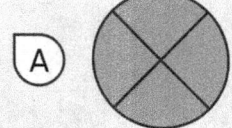

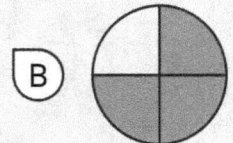

10 Which picture shows a whole?

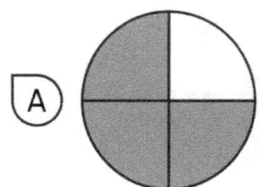 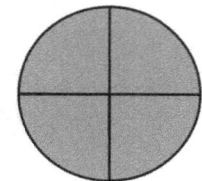 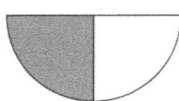

11 Select the rectangle which is shaded $\frac{2}{2}$

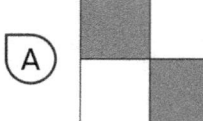 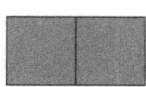 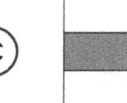

12 Choose the picture which is not shaded $\frac{2}{1}$

 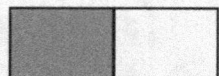  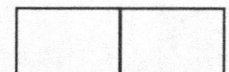

13 Sarah has 3 parrots in a cage. She wants to sell one parrot to her friend. What fraction represents the parrots currently in the cage?

A. $\frac{3}{1}$ B. $\frac{1}{3}$ C. $\frac{1}{1}$ D. $\frac{3}{3}$

14 Daniel has two apples. Each apple was cut into 4 pieces.
He ate $\frac{8}{8}$ of apples. Is he correct or not?

_____

15 Alan cut the dragon fruit into two pieces and gave them to his brother and sister. What fraction of dragon fruit does he give to his brother and sister?

_____

16 True or False. $\frac{3}{1}$ means we have 2 wholes.

(A) True   (B) False

17 Choose the circle partitioned into 10 equal shares and shades $\frac{10}{10}$.

(A)    (B) 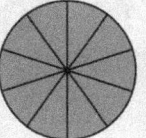   (C)

7.3 Wholes

18 What fraction do we need to make the whole circle shaded?

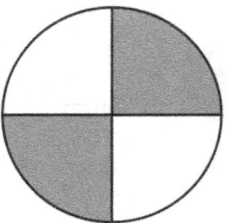

_____

19 Find the value of $\frac{2}{4} + \frac{2}{4} =$?

(A) 1   (B) 4   (C) 8   (D) 16

20 Does the dot represent $\frac{2}{2}$?

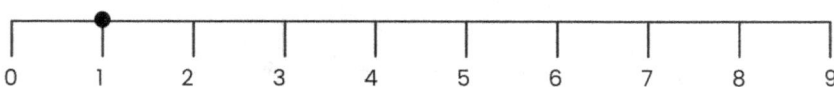

(A) Yes   (B) No

Next Section: Chapter Review 〉〉

1 Jerry cut the cake into three equal shares.
Which option describes the shares?

(A) Halves   (B) One-third   (C) Two-thirds   (D) Thirds

2 Shade two-thirds of the circle.

3 Show fourths inside the rectangle.

4 How would you describe the shaded part of the circle?

_____

5 Where is $\frac{5}{5}$ in this number line?

7.4   Chapter Review

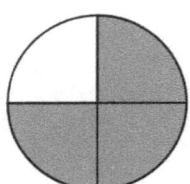

6 _____ of the circle is shaded.

7 _____ of the rectangle is shaded.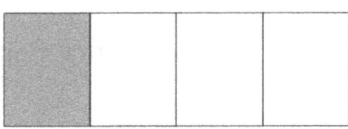

8 How many parts are shaded? 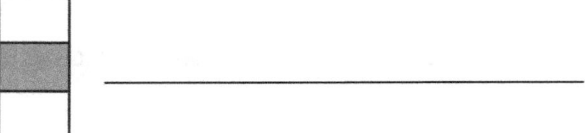 _____

9 How is this shape divided? 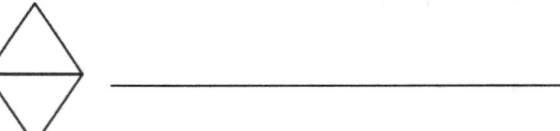 _____

10 **Yes or No.** Do these shapes represent the same fraction?

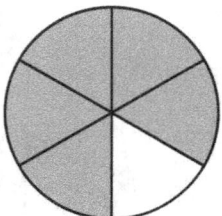 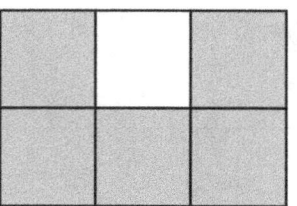 _____

11 What fraction of these animals are a dog?

_____

12 Partition the heart into halves.

13 **True or False:**
The rhombus is partitioned into four equal parts, and $\frac{4}{4}$ are shaded.

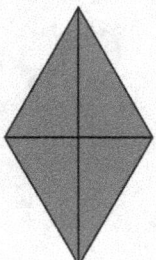 _____

7.4   **Chapter Review**

14 Partition the circle into 12 equal parts.

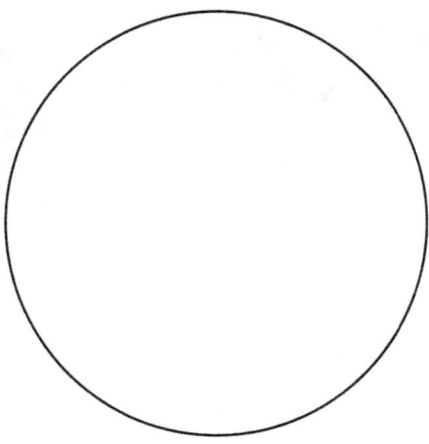

15 Select the whole shaded rectangle.

(A)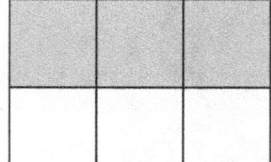

(B)

(C)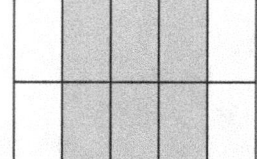

(D)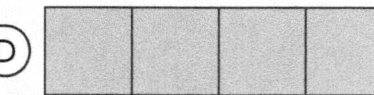

16 Donald has 5 notebooks.

(A) $\frac{5}{10}$ (B) $\frac{5}{5}$ (C) $\frac{1}{5}$ (D) $\frac{5}{1}$

17 Bristol cut a cucumber into 15 pieces.

(A) $\frac{15}{15}$ (B) $\frac{1}{15}$ (C) $\frac{15}{1}$ (D) $\frac{5}{15}$

18 Which number line represents $\frac{9}{9}$?

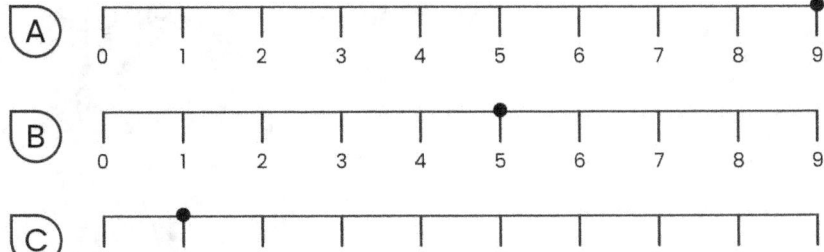

19 Choose the pictures which are not shaded $\frac{4}{1}$

(A)

(B)

(C)

7.4 Chapter Review

20 Find the value of $\frac{1}{3} + \frac{2}{3} = ?$

(A) 0   (B) 2   (C) 3   (D) 1

Next Chapter:
Comprehensive Assessment

COMPREHENSIVE ASSESSMENTS

1 A farmer needs to bring 100 vegetables to the market. He picked 43 tomatoes and 31 potatoes. How many more vegetables does he need for the market? He needs_____more vegetables.

2 Sam is writing a repeated addition equation to go with his picture. How many times does he need to add the number 3? _____.

3 The expression 600 + 50 + 3 is the expanded form of what number? How do you know?

_____

4 Ryan says in order to compare the numbers 883 and 644, you should look at the digit in the tens place. Do you agree or disagree? Why?

_____

5 Which is the best estimate for the length of a moving truck?

Ⓐ 15 yards   Ⓑ 15 inches

Ⓒ 15 miles   Ⓓ 15 centimeters

6 James, a sailboat is 17 feet long. Andy's sailboat is 3 feet longer. Who has the longest sailboats?

(A) James   (B) Andy

7 How many hundreds are in the number 375?

(A) 0   (B) 3   (C) 4   (D) 5

8 Mike is counting by 5's. What should he say after 555?

(A) 560   (B) 575   (C) 525   (D) 580

9 John weighs 60 kilograms, Amy weighs 55 kilograms, and Becky weighs 80 kilograms.
Together, all three children weigh 195 kilograms.

(A) True   (B) False

10 Mike's flower shop is packing flowers for an order. They packed 50 yellow flowers, 8 red flowers, and 5 bundles of orange flowers. Each bundle has 15 flowers in it. How many flowers have they packed?
They packed _____ flowers.

11 Mike has 150 marbles. Sam has 110 more marbles.
How many marbles does Sam have?

(A) 260   (B) 210   (C) 230   (D) 215

12 James has 853 pennies in his piggy bank.
How can he write this number in expanded form?

_____

13 Describe a strategy you would use to add these numbers.
570 + 120 = ?

_____

14 Victoria describes the strategy she uses to subtract these two numbers. 77 - 24 = ?

"First, I round the numbers in the tens place to the nearest ten.
Next, I subtract the numbers in the ones place.
Then, I subtract my answers.
Last, since I rounded my first number up, I have to subtract."

Do you agree with Victoria's strategy? Explain your reasoning.

_____

15 Shack is counting by ones.
What number does he say is directly before 859?

(A) 858   (B) 788   (C) 856   (D) 867

16 Robert is 170 cm tall. Charles is 7 cm taller than Robert.
True or False: Charles is 177 cm tall.

(A) True   (B) False

17 In the first half of the football game, we scored 62 points.
In the second half, we scored 21 points.
What is the total number of points we scored?

(A) 83   (B) 89   (C) 95   (D) 80

18 Fedrick is thinking of a number that is 5 more than 18 minus 4.
What number is Fedrick thinking of?

(A) 18   (B) 16   (C) 19   (D) 25

19 Sam's farm is 1826 meters wide. Mike's farm is 2265 meters wide.
How wide are their two farms put together?

(A) 4091 meters   (B) 5520 meters

(C) 4450 meters   (D) 3520 meters

20 Allen partitioned a rectangle into 5 columns. He wants to make 50 units. How many rows does he need to make?

(A) 6 rows   (B) 10 rows   (C) 4 rows   (D) 7 rows

21 Jim picked a random number which is 2571.
Did he pick an even or odd number?

(A) Even   (B) Odd

22 Is 4 more than 220 an even number or an odd number?

(A) Even   (B) Odd

23 Is the total sum of 1090 and 1102 an even or odd number?

(A) Even   (B) Odd

24 Use mental math to add or subtract 10 to solve the problem.
Andrew has 52 maths books and gives 15 books to his friend. How many books does Andrew have?

(A) 67   (B) 45   (C) 37   (D) 52

25 Write whether the correct or incorrect symbol is used.
975 < 1005.

(A) Correct   (B) Incorrect

26 **Use mental math to add or subtract 100 to solve the problem.**
Tim has 500 pounds. Becky has 100 pounds less than Tim.
How many pounds does Becky have?

(A) 400   (B) 300   (C) 600   (D) 800

27 There are 2564 people in a stadium. What number is in the thousand's place? What number is in the hundreds place? What number is in the tens place? What number is in the ones place?

_____ Thousands _____ Hundreds _____ Tens _____ Ones

28 Decide if the event happens in the A.M. or P.M.
Circle the correct answer. Breakfast

(A) 8:00 A.M.   (B) 8:00 P.M.

29 An apple juice costs $3.35. Sushi has 6 quarters.
Does he have enough money to buy an apple juice?

(A) Yes   (B) No

30 Maria gave $\frac{1}{4}$ of pie to her brother Alan.
How much pie does Maria have left?

_____

31 Sana has 4 parrots in a cage. What fraction shows how many parrots are in the cage?

(A) $\frac{4}{1}$　　(B) $\frac{1}{4}$　　(C) $\frac{1}{1}$　　(D) $\frac{4}{4}$

32 Steve cut the cupcake into three equal parts and ate one part. What fraction of cupcakes was left?

(A) Whole　(B) Two parts　(C) Three parts　(D) Four parts

33 Identify a shape with 2 faces, 0 edges, and 0 vertices.

_____

34 How many vertices does the following shape have?

_____

35 State True or False. A pentagon is 2 dimensional.

(A) True   (B) False

36 Matt drew a shape with 2 corners, 1 straight side, and 1 curved line. What shape did he draw?

(A) Semicircle   (B) Cone   (C) Circle   (D) Sphere

37 In a marriage hall, there were 300 men, 150 women, 100 olderly people and 110 kids. How many people were there in total?

(A) 600   (B) 660   (C) 550   (D) 750

38 Draw a picture using base ten blocks to represent the additional problem. Use the picture to solve the word problem.
In a group of people, 105 ordered noodles, and 123 ordered pasta. How many orders are there in total?

(A) 228   (B) 250   (C) 280   (D) 295

39 Use the counting up and counting down strategies.
Aaron is 10 years old. His sister Kim is double his age. How old is Kim?

(A) 20   (B) 24   (C) 28   (D) 15

40 Draw a picture using base ten blocks to represent the addition problem, then solve the problem. 5895 + 1056 = ?

_____

41 Draw a picture using base ten blocks to represent the addition problem, then solve the problem. 355 + 255 = ?

(A) 610   (B) 720   (C) 727   (D) 736

42 Use the make an equation and then draw picture strategies to solve the one-step word problem with addition and subtraction. Tom bought two gold chains for 5120 dollars. The first chain is 3336 dollars. What is the price of the second chain?

(A) 2000   (B) 1784   (C) 1902   (D) 1951

247

Use regrouping to solve the subtraction equations and the word problem.

43 In a box, there are 650 figs. 315 fig is labeled and the remaining figs are not labeled. How many figs are not labeled in the box?

(A) 335　　(B) 415　　(C) 315　　(D) 450

44 There were 120 parrots in a cage. Stella bought and let 15 parrots free. How many parrots were still in the cage?

(A) 105　　(B) 93　　(C) 81　　(D) 91

45 There are 100 students in a class. Out of that 17 are from a Hostel. How many students do not come from a hostel?

(A) 83　　(B) 79　　(C) 74　　(D) 75

Next Chapter: Assessment 2 ≫

ASSESSMENT 2

COMPREHENSIVE ASSESSMENTS

1 I am thinking of a three-digit number that has 4 ones, 5 hundreds, and 3 tens. What number am I thinking of? How do you know?

_____

2 Celsia has 417 apples. She plucks 15 more from the tree. How many apples does she have now? How do you know?

_____

3 Aaron read 7 chapters of his book. He has 8 more chapters to read. How many chapters are in his book?

(A) 15   (B) 12   (C) 10   (D) 17

4 Use mental math. Mr. Stephen spends $330 over five days. He spends $120 on Monday, and $120 on Tuesday.
How much money does he spend on the other days?
$_____.

5 One box is 50 cm tall. Another box is 15 cm tall. How tall will the boxes be if you stack them on top of each other?

(A) 55   (B) 65   (C) 50   (D) 67

6 Which shape is 2 dimensional?

(A) Triangle   (B) Triangular prism

(C) Cube   (D) Sphere

7 Carol's family has driven 723 miles. Write this number in word form.

_____

8 Tim is trying to write the following comparison. "Five hundred eighty-one is greater than three hundred twenty-two."
Help him write the comparison using numbers and < or > symbols.

_____

9 Linda put her books into 3 columns and 3 rows.
How many books does Linda have?
She has _____ books.

10 Write the number that is equal to 4 hundreds and 6 tens.

_____

11 Which symbol goes in the blank to make the statement true?
5 hundreds and 7 tens _____ 507.

(A) <   (B) >   (C) =   (D) !

12 There are 21 rubber ducks in a box. Seventeen children take one rubber duck each. How many rubber ducks are still in the box?

(A) 6   (B) 4   (C) 10   (D) 15

13 True or False: Thirty-four centimeters is a good estimate for the length of an ear of corn.

(A) True   (B) False

14 John, Jim, and Jill are playing a video game.
John scores 12 points more than Jim. Jim scores 43 points.
Jill scores 15 points more than John. How many points did Jill score?_____points

15 Steve's ice cream cone is 10 inches tall. Tom's ice cream cone is 3 inches shorter than Steve's. Allen's ice cream cone is 2 inches longer than Steve's. Who has the shortest ice cream cone?

(A) Steve   (B) Tom   (C) Allen

16 Yesterday I had 1,100 grams of cookies. Becky ate 600 grams of my cookies and Aaron ate 300 grams of my cookies.
How many grams of cookies do I have left?

_____grams

17 Draw a picture of a ruler to help solve the additional problems with length. In addition moves to the right (toward larger numbers on the ruler).

20 inches + 15 inches = _____inches.

- A) 35 inches
- B) 45 inches
- C) 51 inches
- D) 60 inches

18 Kiraz's dad asks her to think of something that is a centimeter long. What is something that is a centimeter long?

_____.

19 Estimate the length, width, or height of the item.
How long do you think a towel is?

- A) 5 feet
- B) 15 feet
- C) 14 feet
- D) 25 feet

20 What are shorter 25 feet or 25 yards?

_____

21 Eda added 3 columns to the rectangle below.
How many units are in this rectangle after adding in the units?

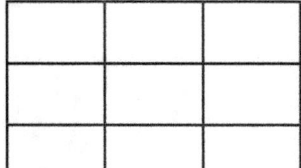

(A) 12 units   (B) 24 units

(C) 18 units   (D) 16 units

22 Robert arranges his books into 3 rows with 2 books in each row.
How many books does he has? _____ books.

23 Write the expanded form of the number. 335.

(A) 300+90+7=335   (B) 300+30+5=335

(C) 700+60+3=335   (D) 500+90+3=335

24 Write the correct symbol in the middle of the two
numbers to correctly compare the numbers.

6352 _____ 5222

(A) <   (B) >   (C) =

25 Use mental math to solve the problems.

1165 – 10 = _____.

(A) 1155   (B) 1142   (C) 1135   (D) 1111

---

26 Rose is working on a math problem.

Eight thousand _____ twenty – five = 8325.

What is missing from the number name?

Explain how Siena can figure out what is missing.

(A) Five hundred   (B) Six Hundred

(C) Three Hundred   (D) Eight Hundred

---

27 $0.44 is the money Zenas has saved. Zenas's father gives her 50 more cents. How much money does Zenas have now?

(A) 0.66   (B) 0.94   (C) 0.85   (D) 0.78

---

28 Stephen watches TV for 1 hour. This clock shows the time he starts watching TV. What is the time shown on the clock?

(A) 3:00   (B) 3:05

(C) 3:10   (D) 3:20

---

29 Ms. Rosy bought a pack of pens that costs $4.55. She gave the clerk 5 one-dollar bills.

How much change will she get back? _____

30 A cookie costs 15¢ each. A chocolate cost 20¢ each. Vensia has 2 quarters, 2 dimes, and 2 pennies. Does she have enough money to buy two cookies and two chocolates?

(A) Yes   (B) No

31 Jerry cut the cake into three equal shares. Which option describes the shares?

(A) Halves   (B) One-third

(C) Two-thirds   (D) Thirds

32 **True or False.** $\frac{3}{1}$ means we have 2 whole.

(A) True   (B) False

33 Rock cut a watermelon into 10 pieces.

(A) $\frac{1}{10}$ (B) $\frac{5}{10}$ (C) $\frac{10}{1}$ (D) $\frac{10}{10}$

34 Draw a closed shape with 4 sides.

35 What shape has curves and circular faces on top and bottom?

_____

36 What shape will be formed when a triangle and an inverted triangle are combined?

_____

37 Draw the shape of a diamond.

38 Eda was making a shape to be presented to her brother as a gift. She first made a shape with four sides and four corners and then inscribed a shape inside it with no edges and vertices. What will be the shape of the gift?

_____

39 How many edges are there for a cuboid?

_____

40 Draw a closed shape with 3 sides

41 Use the counting up and counting down strategies.
Shirley has 55 figs, then she gets 20 more figs from her mom.
How many figs does she have now?

(A) 70   (B) 85   (C) 82   (D) 75

42 Add together the two and three-digit numbers to solve the word problems.
Robert has 46 yellow ribbons and 56 red ribbons. How many ribbons does Robert have in total?

(A) 126   (B) 149   (C) 102   (D) 115

43 Helen has checked out 50 books from the library.
She just finished reading 15 books. How many books does she have left to read?

Ⓐ 38　　Ⓑ 35　　Ⓒ 40　　Ⓓ 33

44 Use regrouping to solve the subtraction equation and the word problem.
In a group of 650 people, 500 people loved coffee, and the other group loved tea. How many people loved tea?

Ⓐ 130　　Ⓑ 233　　Ⓒ 150　　Ⓓ 215

45 Use regrouping to solve the subtraction equations and the word problem.
Sherin has 455 bottles. Linda has 155 bottles. How many more bottles does Sherin have than Linda?

Ⓐ 200　　Ⓑ 236　　Ⓒ 300　　Ⓓ 150

Next Chapter:
Answers and Explanations ≫

ANSWERS AND EXPLANATIONS

TABLE OF CONTENTS

TABLE OF CONTENTS

1. ADDITION AND SUBTRACTION

1.1 ADDITION AND SUBTRACTION FLUENCY

(Use the counting-up strategy to solve the problem.)
1. Answer: A
Explanation: Shiny has 5 apples and got 6 more apples, so 5 + 6 = 11. Now Shiny has 11 apples.

2. Answer: C
Explanation: Madison has 10 cars and buys 7 more cars, so 10 + 7 = 17. Now Madison has 17 cars.

(Use the counting-down strategy to solve the problem.)
3. Answer: B
Explanation: There are 50 students and 7 leave, so 50 - 7 = 43. Now 43 students are remaining in the museum.

4. Answer: A
Explanation: Alen is 23 years old and Cady is 5 years younger (less) than Alen, so 23-5=18. Cady's age is 18 years.

(Use the counting-up strategy to solve the problem.)
5. Answer: B
Explanation: Benny is 31 years old and Brigette is 5 years older (more) than Benny, so 31 + 3 = 34. Brigette's age is 34 years.

6. Answer: B
Explanation: The sum of 6 and 10 (6+10=16).

(Use the counting-down strategy to solve the problem.)
7. Answer: B
Explanation: Ms. Frederick brought 31 sandwiches for lunch. 8 of them were taken, so (31 - 8 = 23). So, 23 sandwiches were packed.

(Use the counting-down and then up strategy to solve the problem.)
8. Answer: A
Explanation: Jim had 19 boxes,1 lost, and then he got 4 more, (19 - 1 + 4 = 22). So, Jim had 22 boxes.

(Use the counting-up strategy to solve the problem.)
9. Answer: B
Explanation: Jeana had 5 roses. She picked 21 lily flowers from her garden. Sushi gave 13 yellow flowers to Jeana. (5 + 21 + 13 = 39). So, Jeana had 39 flowers total.

(Use the counting-up strategy to solve the problem.)
10. Answer: C
Explanation: In a box, there are 25 red and black balls. The box has 7 red balls. (25 - 7 = 18). So, there are 18 black balls.

11. Answer: D
Explanation: Joe has 12 ribbons. Mia gave Joe 13 more ribbons. (12 + 13 = 25). So, Joe has 25 ribbons.

12. Answer: A
Explanation: Pizza Hut has sold 63 pizzas today. They still have 57 pizzas left to sell. (63 + 57 = 120). So, they started with 120 pizzas.

(Use the counting-down and then up a strategy to solve the problem.)
13. Answer: A
Explanation: Mary had 27 peaches and gave 12 peaches to her friend. Also gave 6 it to her mother. Shelly gave 3 peaches to Mary. (27 - 12 - 6 + 3 = 12) So, Mary has 12 peaches remaining.

14. Answer: C
Explanation: Use the counting-up and down strategy to solve the problem.

(Use the counting-up strategy to solve the problem.)
15. Answer: C
Explanation: (15+18=33). So, 33 sandwiches in total.

16. Answer: B
Explanation: There are 87 monkeys in a zoo. 9 were sold off. (87 - 9 = 78). So, 78 monkeys were left.

(Use the counting-down and then up strategy to solve the problem.)
17. Answer:B
Explanation: Mini had 2 cups and then got 9 from Nancy. She had to give 5 it to her neighbor. (2+9-5=6). So, Mini had 6 cups left.

18. Answer: D
Explanation: (13 - 0 + 11 = 24).

(Use the counting-up strategy to solve the problem.)
19. Answer: B
Explanation: (10+3=13). So, Rina drew 13 pictures in total.

(Use the counting-down strategy to solve the problem.)
20.Answer: C
Explanation: Andrew had 10 bananas. He fed 2 to a monkey. (10 - 2 = 8). So, Andrew has 8 bananas left.

1.2 ADDITION OF TWO AND THREE-DIGIT NUMBERS

(Try to answer the question by memory or in your head. If you need help, use the counting up (addition) or counting down (subtraction) strategies to solve the problem.)

1. Answer: B
Explanation: (17 + 21 = 38). So, Lynton has 38 balls in total.

2. Answer: C
Explanation: (27 + 10 = 37). So, Madlyn has 37 apples in total.

3. Answer: B
Explanation: (57 + 21 + 10 + 33 = 121).

4. Answer: C
Explanation: There are 15 monkeys, 23 elephants, 9 Lions, and 47 deer in a zoo (15 + 23 + 9 + 47 = 94). So, there are 94 animals in total.

5. Answer: A
Explanation: The shop has 57 onion baskets and 62 potato baskets.(57 + 62 = 119). So, there are 119 baskets in total.

6. Answer: D
Explanation: Rachel has 129 pies. He buys 20 pies. (129 + 20 = 149). So, there are 149 pies left.

7. Answer: B
Explanation: There are 107 children playing in the park. 25 come to the park later, (107 + 25 = 132). So, there are 132 children altogether in the park.

8.Answer: A
Explanation: Teddy has 119 coins and Marlin received 231 coins (119 + 231 = 350). So, they have 350 coins in total.

9. Answer: A
Explanation: Vertically line up the numbers you are adding, so that each place value is in the same vertical line. Start adding with the one's place value and move to the large place values.

10. Answer: C
Explanation: Vertically line up the numbers you are adding, so that each place value is in the same vertical line. Start adding with the one's place value and move to the large place values.

11. Answer: C
Explanation: Jim has 455 chicks. He buys 551 more chicks. (455 + 551 = 1006). So, Jim has 1006 chicks in total.

(**Vertically line up the numbers you are adding, so that each place value is in the same vertical line. Start adding with the one's place value and move to the large place values.**)

12. Answer: A
Explanation: Calvin had 27 cards with him, Edwin had 25 cards. (27 + 25 = 52). So, there are 52 cards in total.

13. Answer: D
Explanation: Kenny has 223 milk chocolates, Teddy has 115 dark chocolates and Simon has 133 wafer chocolates (223 + 115 + 133 = 471). So, they have 471 chocolates altogether.

14. Answer: C
Explanation: Two of the tickets cost 125 pounds each and the other two tickets cost is 150 pounds., (125 + 125 + 150 + 150 = 550)So, the total cost is 550 pounds.

15. Answer: C
Explanation: Aden has 3 boxes of crackers. There are 200 crackers in each box (200 + 200 + 200 = 600) So, Aden has 600 crackers in total.

16. Answer: B
Explanation: At an aquarium, there are 53 catfish and 21 dolphins. (53 + 21 = 74). There are 74 fishes in the aquarium.

17. Answer: A
Explanation: Augustin has 215 stamps. He collects 55 stamps from his mother and 102 from his cousins. (215 + 55 + 102 = 372) So, Augustin has 372 stamped with him.

18. Answer: C
Explanation: Andres, Mike, Joe, and Mary all have 160 books each (160 + 160 + 160 + 160 = 640) So, they have 640 books altogether.

19. Answer: B
Explanation: Lavinia had 450 guests visiting from her side and Carol had 290 guests visiting from her side. Also, 350 kids were planning to attend the party. (450 + 290 + 350 = 1090) So, they have 1090 guests altogether.

20.Answer: C
Explanation: (35 + 353 = 388).

1.3 SUBTRACTION OF TWO AND THREE-DIGIT NUMBERS

(**Start by subtracting in the ones place value. Then, move to the larger place values. Regroup tens into one's and hundreds into tens when needed.**)

1. Answer: A
Explanation: Start by subtracting in the ones place value. Then, move to the larger place values. Regroup tens into ones and hundreds into tens when needed

2. Answer: B
Explanation: Andrew and Frederick had 836 blackboards. They gave 515 blackboards to an orphanage. (836 - 515 = 321). So, they have 321 blackboards remaining.

3. Answer: C
Explanation: There are 83 students in a class. Out of that 19 are from a Hostel. (83-19=64) So, 64 students come from home.

4. Answer: D
Explanation: In a supermarket, there are 965 boxes to be delivered. On Monday they delivered 113 boxes and on Tuesday they delivered 335 boxes. (965-113-335=517) So, 517 boxes are still to be delivered.

5. Answer: B
Explanation: Bob bought 37 candies. Out of these, he gave 9 to his sister. (37-9=28) So, 28 candies are left with Bob.

6. Answer: A
Explanation: Cathy's mom is 45 years old. Cathy and her age difference is 23. (45 - 23 = 22). So, Cathy's age is 22 years.

7. Answer: D
Explanation: Rio has 121 garlands with him. Edison has 43 fewer garlands than Rio. (121 - 43 = 78). So, Edison has 78 garlands.

8. Answer: C
Explanation: Alisa spends 70 dollars on groceries and 25 dollars on vegetables. (70 - 25 = 45). So, Alisa spends 45 dollars for other groceries.

9. Answer: D
Explanation: There were 107 parrots in a cage. Shiny gave 16 parrots to her friend. (107 - 16 = 91). So, there were 91 parrots still in the cage.

10. Answer: B
Explanation: Vinci has 413 batches. Allen has more batches than Vinci. Together they have 900 batches. (900 - 413 = 487). So, Allen had 487 batches.

11. Answer: C
Explanation: There are 881 packages in a factory. They sell 425 packages. (881 - 425 = 456) So, there are 456 packages left in the factory.

12. Answer: D
Explanation: In a box, there are 850 apples. 333 apples are labeled. (850 - 333 = 517) So, there are 517 apples unlabeled.

13. Answer: 540 and 447
Explanation: Rapunzel has 5 boxes of spaghetti. There are 108 spaghetti in each box.(108 + 108 + 108 + 108 + 108 = 540). She cooks and eats 93 of the spaghetti (540 - 93 = 447). So, Rapunzel has 447 spaghetti remaining

14.Answer: 165 and 72
Explanation: Lisa and Adam have 187 flowers. They give 22 of them to their family. (187-22=165). They give 93 of them to their friends(165-93=72).
So, Lisa and Adam have 72 flowers remaining.

15. Answer: C
Explanation: There are 232 women at the stadium. If there are a total of 450 people at the stadium. (450 - 232 = 218)
So, there are 218 men in the stadium.

16. Answer: B
Explanation: Sherlyn has 567 bottles. Linda has 331 bottles. (567 - 331 = 236)
So, Sherlyn has 236 bottles more than Linda.

17. Answer: C
Explanation: Judith weighs 81 lbs. and Mabel is 21 lbs less than Judith. (81 - 21 = 60)
So, Mabel weighs 60 lbs.

18. Answer: C
Explanation: There are 57 dishes to clean. Jason cleaned 16 dishes. (57-16=41)
So, 41 dishes need to be cleaned.

19. Answer: C
Explanation: Mercy had 133 earrings to be sold in a month. At the end of the month, she had 77 earrings remaining. (133-77=56)
So, 56 earrings were sold.

20. Answer: D
Explanation: In a group of 770 people, 555 people loved coffee and the other group loved tea. (770-555=215)
So, 215 people loved tea.

1.4 WORD PROBLEMS INVOLVING ADDITION AND SUBTRACTION

(Start by adding or subtracting in the ones place value. Then, move to the larger place values. Regroup tens into one's and hundreds into tens when needed.)

1.   Answer: B
Explanation: Amelia has 23 Balls. 7 of them are small rubber balls. (23 - 7 = 16) So, Amelia has 16 smiley balls.

2.   Answer: C
Explanation: Kristen had 57 mangoes. She bought 15 more mangoes (57 + 15 = 72) So, Kristen has 72 mangoes.

3.   Answer: C
Explanation: There is a box of 100 ice cream bars. The box has 44 chocolate ice cream bars (100 - 44 = 56) So, the box has 56 vanilla flavored ice-bars.

4.   Answer: C
Explanation: A garden has 103 rose plants, 99 lemon plants, 50 lily plants, and 176 crotons. (103 + 99 + 50 + 176 = 428)
So, there are total 428 plants in the garden.

5.   Answer: A
Explanation: John's sandwich shop has sold 53 sandwiches today. They still have 79 sandwiches to sell. (53 + 79 = 132) So, they started with 132 sandwiches.

6.   Answer: B
Explanation: Judith has 5 boxes. The first 3 boxes have 11 Choco sticks. The last 2 boxes have 25 Choco sticks. (11+11+11+25+25=83) So, Judith had 83 Choco sticks in total.

7.   Answer: C
Explanation: In a theater, there were 500 seats. 112 were occupied by staff and 203 were occupied by children.(500-112-203=185) So, there were 185 seats vacant for the parents.

8.   Answer: B
Explanation: Becky's grandmother gave her 135 rubber bands. Her dad gave her 93 rubber bands more. Becky gave 13 each to her two brothers. (135+93-13-13=202) So, Becky had 202 rubber bands.

9.   Answer: B
Explanation: On a school bus, there were 37 children going to school. At a stop, some more children got on the bus. Then there were 66 children altogether in the bus. (66-37=29) So, 29 children got into the bus from the stop.

10. Answer: A
Explanation: Haden has taken 31 books from the library. He just finished reading 13 books. (31-13=18) So, Haden has 18 books left to read.

11. Answer: B
Explanation: Sierra walks 1047 meters in a week. She walks 315 fewer meters the next week. (1047-315=732) So, Sierra walks 732 meters the next week.

12. Answer: B
Explanation: The first friend gives 67 gift boxes, the second friend gives 43 gift boxes, the third friend gives 75 gift boxes, and the fourth friend gifts 36 gift boxes (67+43+75+36=221) So, altogether they gave 221 gift boxes.

13. Answer: 180 and 117 bottles
Explanation: Mercy has 5 boxes of cool drinks. Each box has 36 bottles. (36 + 36 + 36 + 36 + 36 = 180) There are 180 bottles together. Also, Mercy sells 63 bottles, (180 - 63 = 117) So, Mercy has been left with 117 bottles.

14. Answer: 64 and 121 cars
Explanation: Tyron has 89 cars in his garage. He repairs 25 cars. (89 - 25 = 64) He receives 57 more cars, (64 + 57 = 121) So, Tyron has been left with 121 cars to be repaired.

15. Answer: 1056 and 1154 dollars.
Explanation: Berlin and Benny buy 5 dresses for their family. The rate is 89, 152, 368, 150, 297 dollars. (89+152+368+150+297=1056) Benny adds another dress which is 98 dollars, (1056+98=1154) So, The total bill is 1154 dollars.

16. Answer: A
Explanation: Allen buys 6000 straws for his shop and sells 2336 straws online. (6000-2336=3664) So, Allen has 3664 straws remaining.

17. Answer: B
Explanation: Aaron has 7665 oranges and buys 3154 oranges more. (7665+3154=10,819) So, Aaron has 10,819 oranges with him.

18. Answer: A
Explanation: The lion walks 5687 yards in a day. The tiger walks 4285 yards in a day. (5687-4283=1402) The difference is 1402.

19. Answer: B
Explanation: Bruce's age is 63 years. Cady is 23 years younger than Bruce. Linda is 7 years older than Cady. (63-23+7=47) Linda's age is 47 years.

20. Answer: C
Explanation: Thomas bought two gold chains for 4238 dollars. The first chain costs 2336 dollars. (4238-2336=1902) The price of the second chain is 1902 dollars

1.5 ADDITION WITH REGROUPING

1. Answer: A
Explanation: *Start by adding in the one's place value and then move to the larger place values. Regroup ones into tens and tens into ones when needed when there is a group of 10 or more ones or tens.*

2. Answer: B
Explanation: *Start by adding in the one's place value and then move to the larger place values. Regroup ones into tens and tens into ones when needed when there is a group of 10 or more ones or tens.*

3. Answer: C
Explanation: *Start by adding in the one's place value and then move to the larger place values. Regroup ones into tens and tens into ones when needed when there is a group of 10 or more ones or tens.*

4. Answer: A
Explanation: *Start by adding in the one's place value and then move to the larger place values. Regroup ones into tens and tens into ones when needed when there is a group of 10 or more ones or tens.*

5. Answer: A
Explanation: *Start by adding in the one's place value and then move to the larger place values. Regroup ones into tens and tens into ones when needed when there is a group of 10 or more ones or tens.*

6. Answer: C
Explanation: *Start by adding in the one's place value and then move to the larger place values. Regroup ones into tens and tens into ones when needed when there is a group of 10 or more ones or tens.*

7. Answer: A
Explanation: *Start by adding in the one's place value and then move to the larger place values. Regroup ones into tens and tens into ones when needed when there is a group of 10 or more ones or tens.*
James has 49 Mangoes. Mary has 34 mangoes.

8. Answer:C
Explanation: *Start by adding in the one's place value and then move to the larger place values. Regroup ones into tens and tens into ones when needed when there is a group of 10 or more ones or tens.*
312 + 425 = 737.

9. Answer:A
Explanation: *Start by adding in the one's place value and then move to the larger place values. Regroup ones into tens and tens into ones when needed when there is a group of 10 or more ones or tens.*
Collin has 33 bags of chocolate. Robin has 26 bags of chocolate.

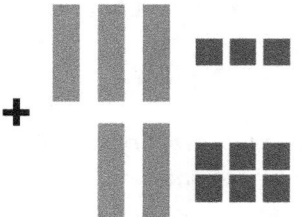

10. Answer: B
Explanation: *Start by adding in the one's place value and then move to the larger place values. Regroup ones into tens and tens into ones when needed when there is a group of 10 or more ones or tens.*
Ashley buys 132 sweet corn today. The next day she buys 323 sweet corn.

11. Answer: B
Explanation: *Start by adding in the one's place value and then move to the larger place values. Regroup ones into tens and tens into ones when needed when there is a group of 10 or more ones or tens.*
There are 3 boxes of ice cream bars in a freezer. There are 135 ice cream in each box.

12. Answer: Incorrect
Explanation: This is incorrect because when you put together the ones there are 8 ones. When you put together the tens there are 5 tens. Write this as the answer in the tens place. When you put the hundred together there are 4 hundreds. Write this as the answer in the hundreds place. The final answer is 458.

13. Answer: Correct
Explanation: This is correct because when you put together the ones there are 7 ones. When you put together the tens there are 4 tens. Write this as the answer in the tens place. When you put together the hundreds there are 3 hundreds. Write this as the answer in the hundreds place. The final answer is 347.

14. Answer: A
Explanation: *Start by adding in the one's place value and then move to the larger place values. Regroup ones into tens and tens into ones when needed when there is a group of 10 or more ones or tens.*
Jerry and Melinda collect 2365 and 1025 stamps.

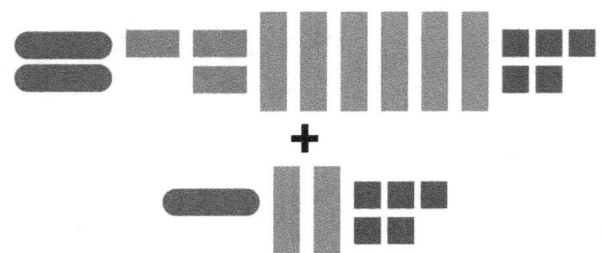

15. Answer: B
Explanation: *Start by adding in the one's place value and then move to the larger place values. Regroup ones into tens and tens into ones when needed when there is a group of 10 or more ones or tens.*
Andrew weighs 53 pounds and his brother weighs 40 pounds.

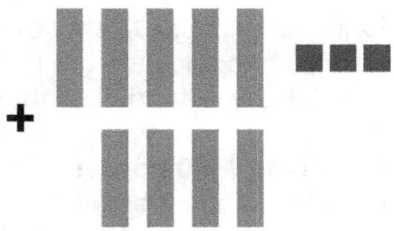

16. Answer: C
Explanation: *Start by adding in the one's place value and then move to the larger place values. Regroup ones into tens and tens into ones when needed when there is a group of 10 or more ones or tens.*
Jane has 3 boxes of lemons. There are 1089 in each box.

17. Answer: B
Explanation: *Start by adding in the one's place value and then move to the larger place values. Regroup ones into tens and tens into ones when needed when there is a group of 10 or more ones or tens.*
Peter owns a restaurant. He buys 2176 coffee bean packs and 1123 tea packs.

18. Answer: A
Explanation: *Start by adding in the one's place value and then move to the larger place values. Regroup ones into tens and tens into ones when needed when there is a group of 10 or more ones or tens.*
There are 190 prisms shaped like cubes and 220 shaped like rectangular prisms.

19. Answer: A
Explanation: *Start by adding in the one's place value and then move to the larger place values. Regroup ones into tens and tens into ones when needed when there is a group of 10 or more ones or tens.*
5269 + 4125 = 9394.

20. Answer: C
Explanation: *Start by adding in the one's place value and then move to the larger place values. Regroup ones into tens and tens into ones when needed when there is a group of 10 or more ones or tens.*
6895 + 1156 = 8051.

1.6 CHAPTER REVIEW

(Use the counting-up the strategy to solve the problem.)
1.   Answer: B
Explanation: Shacks have 65 figs, then she gets 20 more figs, so 65+20=85. Now Shacks has 85 figs.

(Use the counting-down strategy to solve the problem.)
2.   Answer: C
Explanation: There are 90 students and 37 leave, so 90-37=53. Now 53 students are remaining in the class.

(Use the counting-up the strategy to solve the problem.)
3.   Answer: C
Explanation: Mary is 19 years old and Kim is double the age of Mary, so 19+19=38. Kim's age is 38 years.

(Use the counting-down and then up the strategy to solve the problem.)
4.   Answer: B
Explanation: Lucy had 55 burgers. She gave 8 to her friends and then she got 3 more, (55-8+3=50). So, Lucy has 50 burgers.

(Try to answer the question by memory or in your head. If you need help, use the counting up (addition) or counting down (subtraction) strategies to solve the problem.)
5.   Answer: C
Explanation: (26+33=59) So, Cynthia has 59 ribbons in total.

(Try to answer the question by memory or in your head. If you need help, use the counting up (addition) or counting down (subtraction) strategies to solve the problem.)

6. Answer:B
Explanation: There are 63 tomatoes, 55 onions, 29 potatoes, and 47 capsicum in the shop. (63+55+29+47=194) So, there are 194 vegetables in total.

(Vertically line up the numbers you are adding, so that each place value is in the same vertical line. Start adding with the one's place value and move to the large place values.)

7. Answer: A
Explanation: Robin has 6 boxes of plates. There are 300 plates in each box. (300+300+300+300+300+300=1800) So, Robin has 1800 plates in total.

8. Answer: B
Explanation: In a marriage hall, there were 200 men, 250 women, 150 elderly people and 210 kids. (200+250+150+210=810) So, there were 810 guests altogether.

(Start by subtracting the one's place value. Then, move to the larger place values. Regroup tens into ones and hundreds into tens when needed.)

9. Answer: B
Explanation: Matthew had 300 oranges. He sold 75 oranges. (300-75=225) So, Matthew had 225 oranges remaining.

10. Answer: B
Explanation: Raleigh has 360 bags with him. Jack has 127 fewer bags than Raleigh. (360-127=233) So, Jack has 233 bags with him.

11. Answer: 510 and 210
Explanation: Lisa has 2 boxes of toys. There are 255 toys in each box. (255+255=510). She sells 300 toys in online. (510-300=210). So, Lisa has 210 toys remaining.

12. Answer: C
Explanation: There are 2332 girls in a school. If there are a total of 4000 children in the school (4000-2332=1668) So, there are 1668 boys in the school.

13. Answer: A
Explanation: Sherley has 107 chocolates. She bought 25 more chocolates from the market. (107+25=132) So, Sherley has 132 chocolates.

14. Answer: 240 and 140 bottles.
Explanation: Mania has 4 boxes of milk powder. Each box has 60 packs. (60+60+60+60=240) There are 240 packs together. Also, Mania sells 100 pack, (240-100=140) So, Mania has 140 packs left.

15. Answer: B
Explanation: Roger buys 4300 bricks and finds 1055 bricks broken. (4300-1055=3245) So, Roger has 3245 bricks left.

16. Answer: D
Explanation: Lawrence has 2565 apples and buys 3652 apples more from a shopkeeper. (2565+3652=6217) So, Lawrence has 6217 apples with him.

17. Answer: B
Explanation: Start by adding in the one's place value and then move to the larger place values. Regroup ones into tens and tens into ones when needed when there is a group of 10 or more ones or tens.

18. Answer: C
Explanation: Start by adding in the one's place value and then move to the larger place values. Regroup ones into tens and tens into ones when needed when there is a group of 10 or more ones or tens. Alisa has 23 dollars and her friend has 54 dollars.

19. Answer: A
Explanation: Start by adding in the one's place value and then move to the larger place values. Regroup ones into tens and tens into ones when needed when there is a group of 10 or more ones or tens.
135 ordered noodles and 153 ordered pasta.

20. Answer: A
Explanation: Start by adding in the one's place value and then move to the larger place values. Regroup ones into tens and tens into ones when needed when there is a group of 10 or more ones or tens.
2133 + 1243 = 3376.

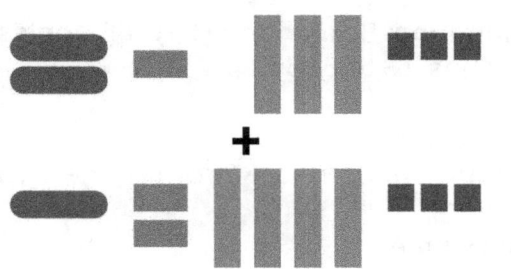

2. FOUNDATIONAL SKILLS FOR MULTIPLICATION

2.1 EVEN AND ODD NUMBERS

1. Answer: A
Explanation: Any number that ends with 1,3,5,7,9 is an odd number. 55 is an odd number.

2. Answer: B
Explanation: Any number that ends with 0,2,4,6,8 is an even number. 36 is an even number.

3. Answer: A
Explanation: It ends with 5. Any number that ends with 1,3,5,7,9 is an odd number.

4. Answer: A
Explanation: Any number that ends with 0,2,4,6,8 is an even number. 48 and 50 are even numbers.

5. Answer: C
Explanation: 15 apples are found in the picture. It ends with 5, so it is an odd number Any number that ends with 1,3,5,7,9 is an odd number.

6. Answer: B
Explanation: The dice shows 4. So it is an even number. Any number that ends with 0,2,4,6,8 is an even number.

7. Answer: D
Explanation: 8 peaches are found in the picture. It is an even number. Any number that ends with 0,2,4,6,8 is an even number.

8. Answer: B
Explanation: The total sum of 75 and 13 is an even number. 75+13=88. It ends with 8, so it is an even number. Any number that ends with 0,2,4,6,8 is an even number.

9. Answer: A
Explanation: Eda had 37 cookies but she lost 8 of them, so 37-8=29. It ends with 9, so it is an odd number. Any number that ends with 1,3,5,7,9 is an odd number.

10. Answer: B
Explanation: The difference between 550 and 230 is an even number. 550-230=320. It ends with 0, so it is an even number. Any number that ends with 0,2,4,6,8 is an even number.

11. Answer: B
Explanation: The number Sushi picked is 5261, which is an odd number. It ends with 1, so it is an odd number. Any number that ends with 1,3,5,7,9 is an odd number.

12. Answer: B
Explanation: The total sum of 1250 and 1001 is an odd number. 1250+ 1001=2251. It ends with 1, so it is an odd number. Any number that ends with 1,3,5,7,9 is an odd number.

13. Answer: B
Explanation: There are 7 students doing collage work together. It is an odd number. Any number that ends with 1,3,5,7,9 is an odd number.

14. Answer: B
Explanation: The total sum of 67 and 68 is an odd number. 67+68=135. It ends with 5, so it is an odd number. Any number that ends with 1,3,5,7,9 is an odd number.

15. Answer: A
Explanation: 5 more than 555 is 560. 560 is an even number because it ends with 0.

16. Answer: 950,952,954,956,958,960
Explanation: Any number that ends with 0,2,4,6,8 is an even number.

17. Answer: 1001,1003,1005,1007,1009.
Explanation: Any number that ends with 1,3,5,7,9 is an odd number.

18. Answer: A
Explanation: The number is 252 and it's an even number because it ends with 2.

19. Answer: B
Explanation: The number is 1291 and it's an odd number because it ends with 1.

20. Answer: B
Explanation: 42 is an even number because it ends with 2.

2.2 INTERPRETING ARRAYS

1. Answer: A
Explanation: A shows 3 rows and 2 columns.

2. Answer: A
Explanation: A shows 2 rows and 5 columns.

3. Answer: A
Explanation: Because there are 4 rows and 4 columns.

4. Answer: 3+3+3
Explanation: She can put the stamps into 3 columns and 3 stamps in each row.

5. Answer: Sam has 30 books
Explanation: 6 + 6 + 6 + 6 + 6 = 30.

6. Answer: A
Explanation: Box A has 5+5+5=15 apples and Box B has 6+6+6+6=24.

7. Answer: B
Explanation: There are 2 rows in the array.

8. Answer: A
Explanation: There are 4 rows in the array.

9. Answer: A
Explanation: 4 + 4 or 2 + 2 + 2 + 2.

10. Answer: C
Explanation: There are a total of 8 smiley faces.

11. Answer: A
Explanation: Chris has 3 rows with 3 cakes in each row.

12. Answer: B
Explanation: 3 + 3 + 3.

13. Answer: A
Explanation: There are 9 cakes with Chris.

14. Answer: B
Explanation: Tom has 3 rows with 4 cakes in each row.

15. Answer: A
Explanation: 4 + 4 + 4.

16. Answer: B
Explanation: There are 12 cakes with Tom.

17. Answer: A
Explanation: Maddy has 4 rows with 5 cakes in each row.

18. Answer: A
Explanation: 5 + 5 + 5 + 5.

19. Answer: D
Explanation: There are 20 cakes with Maddy.

20. Answer: C
Explanation: Chris has 9, Tom has 12, and Maddy has 20 cakes

2.3 CREATING ARRAYS

1. Answer: C
Explanation: Rows go from side to side.

2. Answer: D
Explanation: Rows go from side to side.

3. Answer: B
Explanation: Columns go up and down.

4. Answer: A
Explanation: Rows go from side to side.

5. Answer: B
Explanation: 7 + 7 + 7 + 7 + 7 + 7 = 42.

6. Answer: C
Explanation: 5 + 5 + 5 + 5 + 5 = 25.
Andrew drew a square with 25 units.

7. Answer: D
Explanation: 6 + 6 = 12.
Thomas drew a rectangle with 12 units.

8. Answer: A
Explanation: 6 + 6 + 6 + 6 + 6 = 36.
Eda has to draw a square with 6 rows and 6 columns, so it makes 36 units.

9. Answer: D
Explanation: 5 + 5 + 5 + 5 + 5 + 5 + 5 = 35.
Beldon has to draw a rectangle with 7 rows and 5 columns, so it makes 35 units.

10. Answer: C
Explanation: 3 + 3 + 3 + 3 = 12.
Olivia drew a rectangle with 12 units.

11. Answer: C
Explanation: 6 + 6 + 6 + 6 + 6 = 36
Columns go up and down.

12. Answer: A
Explanation: 2 + 2 + 2 + 2 + 2 + 2 + 2 = 14.
So, Collin has to add 3 more rows to rectangle A to get 14 units.

13. Answer: B
Explanation: 1 + 1 + 1 + 1 + 1 + 1 = 6
So, Elena has to add 2 more row to rectangle B to get 6 units.

14. Answer: A
Explanation: Judy added 2 rows to the rectangle A and 2 columns to the rectangle B
Rectangle A has 2 + 2 + 2 + 2 + 2 + 2 + 2 = 14 and Rectangle B has 4 + 4 + 4 = 12
So, Rectangle A has more units.

15. Answer: A
Explanation: Jack has to add 4 rows to Rectangle A and make 18 units.
Rectangle A has 2+2+2+2+2+2+2+2+2 = 18

16. Answer: C
Explanation: 4 + 4 + 4 + 4 + 4 + 4 + 4 = 28
Allen drew a rectangle with 28 units.

17. Answer: A
Explanation: So, after adding columns Nora has a rectangle with 12 units.

18. Answer: D
Explanation: 5 + 5 + 5 + 5 + 5 + 5 + 5 + 5 = 40
John partitioned a rectangle into 5 rows and 8 columns.

19. Answer: A
Explanation: 6 + 6 + 6 = 18

20. Answer: C
Explanation: 7 + 7 + 7 + 7 = 28
So, after 2 adding rows Peter has a rectangle with 28 units.

2.4 CHAPTER REVIEW

1. Answer: A
Explanation: Any number that ends with 1,3,5,7,9 is an odd number. 103 is an odd number.

2. Answer: B
Explanation: There were 50 students playing at the playground and 10 more students joined them, so 50+10=60. It ends with 0, so it is an even number. Any number that ends with 0,2,4,6,8 is an even number.

3. Answer: B
Explanation: The number is 991 and it's an odd number because it ends with 1. Any number that ends with 1,3,5,7,9 is an odd number.

4. Answer: B
Explanation: The difference between 1030 and 1550 is an even number. 1030 - 1550 = 520. It ends with 0, so it is an even number. Any number that ends with 0,2,4,6,8 is an even number.

5. Answer: B
Explanation: 7 more than 660 is 667. 667 is an odd number because it ends with 7. Any number that ends with 1,3,5,7,9 is an odd number.

6. Answer: C
Explanation: 9 peaches are found in the picture. It is an odd number. Any number that ends with 1,3,5,7,9 is an odd number.

7. Answer: B
Explanation: There are 2 rows in the array.

8. Answer: B
Explanation: There are 3 columns in the array.

9. Answer: A
Explanation: 3+3 is the repeated addition in this array.

10. Answer: A
Explanation: There are 6 shapes.

11. Answer: Mary has 12 books
Explanation: 3 + 3 + 3 + 3 = 12.

12. Answer:A
Explanation: Box A has 4 + 4 + 4 + 4 = 16 chocolates and Box B has 4 + 4 + 4 = 12 Chocolates.

13. Answer: A
Explanation: The number Rocky picked is 2334, which is an even number. It ends with 4, so it is an even number. Any number that ends with 0,2,4,6,8 is an even number.

14. Answer: A
Explanation: Any number that ends with 0,2,4,6,8 is an even number. 98 and 108 are even numbers.

15. Answer: C
Explanation: 4 + 4 + 4 + 4. So, Sarah has to add 1 more row to rectangle B to get 16 units.

16. Answer: C
Explanation:
5 + 5 + 5 + 5 = 20 or 4 + 4 + 4 + 4 + 4 = 20
So, Jenny has to add 2 more rows to rectangle A or 2 more rows to rectangle B to get 20 units.

17. Answer: A
Explanation: Linda has to add 3 rows to Rectangle A and make 25 units.
Rectangle A has 5 + 5 + 5 + 5 + 5 = 25.

18. Answer: B
Explanation: Aaron has to add 3 columns to Rectangle B and make 21 units.
Rectangle B has 7 + 7 + 7 = 21.

19. Answer: D
Explanation: 7 + 7 + 7 + 7 + 7 = 35.
Johnny drew a rectangle with 35 units.

20. Answer: D
Explanation: 6 + 6 + 6 + 6 + 6 + 6 + 6 = 42.
Becky has to draw a rectangle with 6 columns and 7 rows, so it makes 42 units.

3. NUMBERS AND OPERATIONS IN BASE TEN

3.1 PLACE VALUE UP TO THE THOUSANDTHS PLACE

1.   Answer: 2 ones, 5 tens, and 2 hundreds
Explanation: Hundreds - 2; Tens - 5; One's - 2
In the number 252 there is a 2 in the one's place, a 5 in the tens place, and 2 in the hundreds place.

2.   Answer: 3 ones, 0 tens, and 0 hundreds
Explanation: Hundreds - 3; Tens - 0; One's - 0
In the number 30 there is a 3 in the one's place, a 0 in the tens place, and 0 in the hundreds place.

3.   Answer: 528
Explanation: The picture shows 5 hundreds, 2 tens, and 8 ones. This represents 528.

4.   Answer: 570
Explanation: The picture shows 5 hundreds, 7 tens, and 0 ones. This represents 570.

5.   Answer: Picture of 2 hundreds, 1 tens, and 0 ones
Explanation:

6.   Answer: Picture of 1 hundred, 1 tens, and 2 ones
Explanation:

7.   Answer: 32
Explanation: 2 one and 3 tens are equal to 32.

8.   Answer: 7185
Explanation: 5 one and 1 tens 8 hundreds and 7 thousands is equal to 7185.

9.   Answer : Thousands - 9, Hundreds - 8, Tens -7, Ones - 4
Explanation:
In the number, 9874 there is an 9 in the thousands place, 8 in the hundreds place, 7 in the tens place, and 4 in the ones place.

10. Answer : Thousands – 2, Hundreds - 3, Tens - 8, Ones - 8
Explanation:
In the number, 2,388 there is an 8 in the ones place, 8 in the tens place, 3 in the hundred place, and 2 in the thousands place.

11. Answer: B
Explanation: You have to add together the groups of one's (5+2=7), the tens (3+6=9), and the hundreds (2+4=6). Use those digits to make up the final number 697.

12. Answer: D
Explanation: You have to add together the thousands (2+2=4), the hundreds (3+2=5), the tens (4+2=6), and the one's (2+3=5). Use these digits to make the final number 4565.

13. Answer: C
Explanation: You have to add together the thousands (5+2=7), the hundreds (2+3=5), the tens (3+3=6), and the one's (3+6=9). Use these digits to make the final number 7569.

14. Answer: A
Explanation: There is a 1 in the one's place. There are 32 in the tens place, which can be grouped into 3 hundreds and 2 tens. Now there are 6 hundreds. There are 2 thousands. Use these digits to make the final number 2621.

15. Answer: A
Explanation: Use the clues to determine what digits are in the one, tens, hundreds, and thousands places. Put those digits together to make the final number 6335.

16. Answer: 3 ones, 2 tens, and 8 hundreds
Explanation: Hundreds - 8
Tens - 2
Ones - 3
In the number 823 there is a 3 in the ones place, 2 in the tens place, and 8 in the hundreds place.

17. Answer: 4 ones, 2 tens, 2 hundreds, and 1 thousand
Explanation: Thousand - 1 ; Hundreds - 2
Tens - 2 ; Ones - 4
In the number 1224 there is a 4 in the one's place, 2 in the tens place, 2 in the hundreds place and 1 in the thousands place.

18. Answer: Picture of 2 tens, and 0 ones
Explanation: To make the number 20 with base ten blocks use 2 tens.

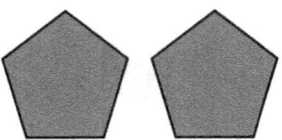

19. Answer: Picture of 1 thousand, 0 hundred, 0 tens, and 0 ones
Explanation: To make the number 1000 with base ten blocks use 1 thousand.

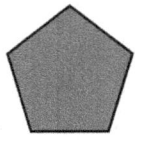

20. Answer: B
Explanation: 6 one's blocks, 5 tens blocks, and 8 hundreds blocks is equal to 856.

3.2 EXPANDED FORM AND NUMBER NAMES

1. Answer: A
Explanation: If you add them together 80+5 it equals 85.

2. Answer: B
Explanation: If you add them together 770+20+3 it equals 793.

3. Answer: A
Explanation: There is 9 in the ten places, which has a value of 90. There is 5 in the ones place, which has a value of 5.

4. Answer:C
Explanation: There is an 8 in the hundreds place, which has a value of 800. There is a 6 in the tens place, which has a value of 60. There is a 2 in the tens place, which has a value of 20.

5. Answer: C
Explanation: There is a 2 in the hundreds place, which has a value of 200. There is a 5 in the tens place, which has a value of 50. There is a 3 in the one's place, which has a value of 3.

6. Answer: D
Explanation: There is a 7 in the thousands place, which has a value of 7000. There is a 8 in the hundreds place, which has a value of 800. There is a 9 in the tens place, which has a value of 90. There is a 0 in the one's places, which has a value of 0.

7. Answer: A
Explanation: There is an 5 in the hundreds place, which has a value of 500. There is a 2 in the tens place, which has a value of 20. There is a 7 in the one's place, which has a value of 7.

8. Answer: C
Explanation: In the number, 4295 there is a 4 in the thousands place, which has a value of 4000. That is the first number that is missing. There is a 9 in the tens place, which has a value of 90. That is the second number that is missing. There is a 5 in the ones place, which has a value of 5. That is the third number that is missing.

9. Answer: A
Explanation: There is a 8 in the hundreds place, which has a value of 800. There is a 5 in the tens place, which has a value of 50. There is a 2 in the ones place, which has a value of 2.

10. Answer: C
Explanation: 4000+600+80+7
There is a 4 in the thousands place, which has a value of 4000. There is a 6 in the hundreds place, which has a value of 600. There is an 8 in the tens place, which has a value of 80. There is a 7 in the one's place, which has a value of 7.

11. Answer: D
Explanation: There is a 5 in the tens place, which has a value of 50. This can be expressed as fifty.

12. Answer: B
Explanation: There is a 6 in the thousands place, which has a value of 6000. This can be expressed as six thousand. There is a 8 in the tens place, which has a value of 80. This can be expressed as eighty.

13. Answer: B
Explanation: There is a 5 in the thousands place, 2 in the hundreds place, 5 in the tens place, and 6 in the one's place.

14. Answer: A
Explanation: There is a 9 in the thousands place, 8 in the hundreds place, 5 in the tens place, and 4 in the one's place.

15. Answer: C
Explanation: Twenty-five
There is an 2 in the tens place, and 5 in the one's place.

16. Answer: B
Explanation: Five thousand seven hundred twenty-one. There is a 5 in the thousands place, 7 in the hundreds place, 2 in the tens place, and a 1 in the one's place.

17. Answer: C
Explanation: Seven hundred seventy-seven. You have to add together the ones (6+1=7), the tens (2+5=7), and the hundreds (4+3=7). Use these digits to make up the final number 777.

18. Answer: D
Explanation: Eight thousand eight hundred sixty-six. You have to add together the ones (1+5=6), the tens (3+3=6), the hundreds (6+2=8), and the thousands (5+3=8). Use these digits to make up the final number 8866.

19. Answer: B
Explanation: There is a 6 in the hundreds place, which has a value of 600. This can be expressed as six hundred. That is the word that is missing.

20. Answer: B
Explanation: Eight thousand three hundred sixty-two
The number is 8362.

> ### 3.3 MENTAL MATH WITH 10S AND 100S

1.   Answer: B
Explanation: Add five to the number in the one's place. The rest of the number stays the same.
Alice has 30 and gets an extra 5, so 30+5=35. Alics has 35 apples.

2.   Answer: A
Explanation: Subtract six from the number in the one's place. The rest of the number stays the same.
Lavina has 678 and gives 6, so 678-6=672. Lavina has 678 bags.

3.   Answer: A
Explanation: Add one to the number in the tens place. The rest of the number stays the same.

4.   Answer: C
Explanation: Subtract one from the number in the tens place. The rest of the number stays the same.

5.   Answer: C
Explanation: Add one to the number in the tens place. The rest of the number stays the same. So, Fionna has (40+10=50) boxes.

6.   Answer: B
Explanation: Subtract one from the number in the tens place. The rest of the number stays the same. So, Jane has (280-10=270) Pencils.

7.   Answer: B
Explanation: Subtract one from the number in the tens place. The rest of the number stays the same. So, Tina and Tim have (707-10=697) cupcakes.

8.   Answer: D
Explanation: Subtract 8 from the hundreds, 9 from the tens, and 0 from the one's place.

9.   Answer: B
Explanation: Add one to the number in the tens place. The rest of the number stays the same. Jerry has 10 more than Roger, so (559+10=569) pipes.

10. Answer: C
Explanation: Subtract one from the number in the tens place. The rest of the number stays the same.

11. Answer: C
Explanation: Add one to the number in the hundreds place. The rest of the number stays the same.

12. Answer: B
Explanation: Subtract one from the number in the hundreds place. The rest of the number stays the same.

13. Answer: C
Explanation: Add one to the number in the hundreds place. The rest of the number stays the same.

14. Answer: A
Explanation: Add one to the number in the hundreds place. The rest of the number stays the same.

15. Answer: A
Explanation: Subtract one from the number in the hundreds place. The rest of the number stays the same.

16. Answer: B
Explanation: Add one to the number in the hundreds place. The rest of the number stays the same.

17. Answer: A
Explanation: Subtract one from the number in the hundreds place. The rest of the number stays the same.

18. Answer: B
Explanation: Add one to the number in the hundreds place. The rest of the number stays the same.

19. Answer: A
Explanation: Subtract one from the number in the hundreds place. The rest of the number stays the same.

20. Answer: A
Explanation: Subtract one from the number in the hundreds place. The rest of the number stays the same.

3.4 COMPARING NUMBERS

1. Answer: B
Explanation: First number and second number are not equal.
Decide if the first number is larger, the second number is larger, or the numbers are the same.

2. Answer: A
Explanation: 615 is the larger number.
Decide if the first number is larger, the second number is larger, or the numbers are the same.

3. Answer: B
Explanation: 950 is less than 1000.
Decide if the first number is larger, the second number is larger, or the numbers are the same.

4. Answer: A
Explanation: *Decide if the first number is larger, the second number is larger, or the numbers are the same.*
170 > 155.

5. Answer: C
Explanation: *Decide if the first number is larger, the second number is larger, or the numbers are the same.*
765 = 765.

6. Answer:B
Explanation: *Decide if the first number is larger, the second number is larger, or the numbers are the same.*
345 < 355.

7. Answer: B
Explanation: 689 is larger.
Decide if the first number is larger, the second number is larger, or the numbers are the same.
675 < 689.

8. Answer: A
Explanation: 517 is larger.
Decide if the first number is larger, the second number is larger, or the numbers are the same.
517 > 500.

9. Answer: C
Explanation: Both the numbers are equal to 566. So, Clady also bought 566 apples.

10. Answer: A
Explanation: Choose a number greater than 140.

11. Answer: B
Explanation: 735 is the larger number.
Decide if the first number is larger, the second number is larger, or the numbers are the same.

12. Answer: B
Explanation: 590 is smaller than 690. It should be 590 < 690.

13. Answer: A
Explanation: 1564 is the larger number.
Decide if the first number is larger, the second number is larger, or the numbers are the same.

14. Answer: B
Explanation: 522 is the larger number.
Decide if the first number is larger, the second number is larger, or the numbers are the same.

15. Answer: B
Explanation: 190 is the larger number.
Decide if the first number is larger, the second number is larger, or the numbers are the same.

16. Answer: C
Explanation: Both the numbers are equal.
Decide if the first number is larger, the second number is larger, or the numbers are the same.

17. Answer: B
Explanation: 547 is the larger number.
Decide if the first number is larger, the second number is larger, or the numbers are the same.

18. Answer: B
Explanation: Five hundred fifty-one is the larger number.
Decide if the first number is larger, the second number is larger, or the numbers are the same.

19. Answer: C
Explanation: Both the numbers are equal.545=545.
Decide if the first number is larger, the second number is larger, or the numbers are the same.

20. Answer: B
Explanation: Sixty hundred sixty three is the larger number.
Decide if the first number is larger, the second number is larger, or the numbers are the same.

1. Answer: A picture of 3 thousands,2 hundreds,2 tens, and 1 ones.

Explanation: In the number 3221 there are 3 thousands,2 hundreds, 2 tens, and 1 ones.

2. Answer: B
Explanation: The picture shows 2 thousands, 4 hundreds, 3 tens, and 4 ones.

3. Answer: C
Explanation: 5 thousand, 4 hundreds, 6 tens, and 2 ones is equal to 5462.

4. Answer: C
Explanation: Add 1 more to the number in the hundreds place. The rest of the number stays the same. Already there are 1004 people, 100 people got added, so (1004+100=1104).

5. Answer: A
Explanation: There is a 6 in the thousands place, which has a value of 6000. There is a 9 in the hundreds place, which has a value of 900. There is a 5 in the tens place, which has a value of 50. There is an 8 in the one's place, which has a value of 8.

6. Answer: A
Explanation: There is an 5 in the hundreds place, which has a value of 500. There is a 2 in the tens place, which has a value of 20. There is a 5 in the one's place, which has a value of 5.

7. Answer: B
Explanation: Add 1 more to the number in the hundreds place. The rest of the number stays the same. Already there are 555 flowers, 100 flowers got added, so (555+100=655).

8. Answer: A
Explanation: Eight thousand four hundred thirty-nine. There is a 8 in the thousands place, which has a value of 8000. This can be expressed as eight thousand. There is a 4 in the hundreds place, which has a value of 400. This can be expressed as four hundred. There is a 3 in the tens place, which has a value of 30. This can be expressed as thirty. There is a 9 in the one's place, which has a value of 9. This can be expressed as nine.

9. Answer: B
Explanation: Add one to the number in the hundreds place. The rest of the number stays the same. Carlos has 790 blocks, so (790+10=800) blocks.

10. Answer: A
Explanation: Add one to the number in the hundreds place. The rest of the number stays the same. Tomy has 10000 blocks, so, (10000+100=10100) blocks.

11. Answer: A
Explanation: Subtract one to the number in the tens place. The rest of the number stays the same. Roger has 110 pieces of paper, so, (110-10=100) pieces of paper.

12. Answer: B
Explanation: Subtract one to the number in the hundreds place. The rest of the number stays the same. Melissa has 100 candles less, so (905-100=805) candles.

13. Answer: D
Explanation: There is a 8 in the hundreds place, which has a value of 800. This can be expressed as eight hundred. That is the word that is missing.

14. Answer: A
Explanation: There are 1 in the ones place. There are 28 in the tens place, which can be grouped into 3 hundreds and 8 tens. Now there are 8 hundreds. There are 5 thousands. Use these digits to make the final number 5838.

15. Answer: A
Explanation: There is a 8 in the hundreds place, which has a value of 800. There is a 3 in the tens place, which has a value of 30. There is a 7 in the one's place, which has a value of 7.

16. Answer: A
Explanation: There is a 6 in the hundreds place, which has a value of 600. There is a 9 in the tens place, which has a value of 90. There is a 7 in the one's place, which has a value of 7.

17. Answer: A
Explanation: The picture shows 5 tens, and 7 ones.

18. Answer: C
Explanation: Subtract one to the number in the tens place. The rest of the number stays the same. Andes has 57 books and 10 are given, so (57-10=47) books.

19. Answer: A picture of 3 hundreds, 1 tens, and 1 ones.

Explanation: In the number 311 there are 3 hundreds, 1 tens, and 1 ones.

20. Answer: A
Explanation: There is a 9 in the thousands place, which has a value of 9000, 1 in the hundreds place, which has a value of 100. There is a 5 in the tens place, which has a value of 50. There is a 3 in the one's place, which has a value of 3.

4. MEASUREMENT AND DATA

4.1 MEASURING LENGTH IN STANDARD UNITS AND METRIC UNITS

1. Answer: A
Explanation: It is easiest to measure small objects (less than 1 foot in length) with a ruler.

2. Answer: A
Explanation: It is easiest to measure small objects (less than 1 foot in length) with a ruler.

3. Answer: A
Explanation: It is easiest to measure small objects (less than 1 foot in length) with a ruler.

4. Answer: C
Explanation: It is easiest to measure larger objects (more than 1 meter/ 100 centimeters) with a measuring tape.

5. Answer: Answers will vary
Explanation: Line the object up on the left side of the ruler at 0. See where the end of the object lines up with the ruler. The number it is closest to is how many inches in length the object is.

6. Answer: Yardstick
Explanation: It is easiest to measure objects between 1 foot and 1 yard (3 feet) in length with a yardstick.

7. Answer: Mary is correct
Explanation: They should use a measuring tape because the path is very long. A measuring tape is much longer than a ruler, so it makes more sense to use the longer tool to measure the length of the path.

8. Answer: A
Explanation: A rose plant measures 15 centimeters tall. The next week it measures 25 centimeters tall. The difference is 10 cm.

9. Answer: Answers will vary
Explanation: Explain how to line the 0 on the ruler up on the side of the trailer. Mark the end of the ruler with your finger or another object. Move the ruler to line up the 0 with your finger or other object. Repeat this process until you get to the end of the trailer. Keep count of how many centimeters or meters you have measured along the way.

10. Answer: Becky is correct
Explanation: They should use a ruler because a chip is very small. A ruler is much smaller than a yardstick, so it makes more sense to use the shorter tool to measure the width of the chip.

11. Answer: They are the same.
Explanation: 100+100+100=300. There are 100 centimeters in each meter. If you add together the centimeters in 3 meters it equals 300 centimeters.

12. Answer: B
Explanation: Kinston is 55 inches tall. Her older brother Gaston is 12 inches taller than Kinston. Adding both we get 67 inches which is the height of Gaston

13. Answer: C
Explanation: The yellow piece of the strip is 31 inches long. The blue piece of the strip is 25 inches long. The Red piece strip is 40 inches long. Adding all strips we get 96 inches which is the length of strips put together.

14. Answer: They are the same
Explanation: There are 100 centimeters in a meter, so 1 meter = 100 cms are the same length. So, 200 cm = 2 m Both Kenny and Lavinia are correct.

15. Answer: They did not get the same measurement
Explanation: A foot is 12 inches long. 14 inches and 12 inches are not the same length.

16. Answer: They are the same
Explanation: There are 12 inches in a foot, so 1 foot = 12 inches So,48 inches = 4 feet. Both construction papers are the same length.

17. Answer: Answers will vary
Explanation: A meter stick is larger than a ruler. A mixing bowl is smaller, but you can still use a meter stick to measure the height of the bowl. Line the mixing bowl up on the 0 on the meter stick. See where the end of the object lines up with the meter stick. The number it is closest to is how many centimeters in length the object is.

18. Answer: C
Explanation: Palona's backyard is 3157 inches wide. Her neighbor's yard is 3365 inches wide Adding both we get 6522 inches which is the width of yards put together.

19. Answer: B
Explanation: Martin's farm is 2826 meters wide. Rosy's farm is 5263 centimeters wide. Adding both we get 8089 meters which is the length of farms put together.

20. Answer: A
Explanation: Pricy draws a red line on the sidewalk with chalk that is 4562 inches long. She also draws a yellow line with chalk. She drew a total of 6823 inches with chalk. The difference is 2261 inches.

4.2 COMPARING LENGTHS IN STANDARD AND METRIC UNITS

1. Answer: Answers will vary
Explanation: Line the object up on the left side of the ruler at 0. See where the end of the object lines up with the ruler. The number it is closest to is how many inches/centimeters in length the object is.

2. Answer: A
Explanation: 10 centimeters is too small for the length of the cucumber. 10 feet and 10 meters are too large for the length of the cucumber.

3. Answer: C
Explanation: 8 inches and 8 centimeters are too small for the height of a broom. 8 yards is too large for the height of a broom.

4. Answer: B
Explanation: 22 inches, 22 yards, and 22 meters are too large for the height of a shampoo bottle.

5. Answer: A
Explanation: Line the object up on the left side of the ruler at 0. See where the end of the object lines up with the ruler. The number it is closest to is how many inches/centimeters in length the object is.

6. Answer: A
Explanation: See how many of an object you are using to measure with fits across the length, width or height of the object you are measuring.

7. Answer: 5 inches
Explanation: Inches are longer than centimeters. The number of units are the same, so 5 inches are longer than 5 centimeters.

8.   Answer: 15 feet
Explanation: Yards are longer than feet. The number of units are the same, so 15 feet is shorter than 15 yards.

9.   Answer: Incorrect
Explanation: Yards are much longer than inches. There are 36 inches in 1 yard. Even though 2 is a smaller number than 8, 2 yards is still longer than 8 inches.

10. Answer: Correct
Explanation: When comparing measurements that use the same units of measurement, you can just analyse which number is larger. 10 is larger than 8, so 10 feet is longer than 8 feet.

11.   Answer: Aaron is correct,
Explanation: 5 feet is too small for the length of a farm house.

12. Answer: 3 meters is the right answer.
Explanation: 3 centimeters and 3 inches are too small for the width of a couch. 3 yards is too large for the width of a couch.

13. Answer: 550 meters
Explanation: Meters are longer than inches.

14.   Answer: Inches are longer than centimeters
Explanation: Inches are longer than centimeters, so when measuring an object with both units of measurement it will take more of the smaller units to fill up the length, width, or height of the object.

15. Answer: Bob's basket is wider, as it is in feet
Explanation: There are roughly 30 centimetres in 1 foot. John's basket is less than 1 foot wide. Bob's basket is 3 feet wide.

16. Answer: A donut is 8 paper clips wide
Explanation: Paper clips are about an inch in length. A guitar is about a yard or meter in length. 8 guitars is too large for the width of a donut.

17. Answer: Feet are longer than centimeters
Explanation: Feet are longer than centimeters.

18. Answer: A
Explanation: Line the object up on the left side of the ruler at 0. See where the end of the object lines up with the ruler. The number it is closest to is how many inches/centimeters in length the object is.

19. Answer: They did not get the same measurement
Explanation: There are 100 centimeters in 1 meter. 187 centimeters and 200 centimeters are not equal.

20. Answer: 10 cm
Explanation: Feet are longer than centimeters.

4.3 ESTIMATING LENGTHS

1.   Answer: C or D
Explanation: *Choose a smaller unit of measurement (inches or centimeters) for small items. Choose a larger unit of measurement (feet or meters) for large items.*

2.   Answer: C or D
Explanation: *Choose a smaller unit of measurement (inches or centimeters) for small items. Choose a larger unit of measurement (feet or meters) for large items.*

3.   Answer: C
Explanation: *Choose which unit of measurement to use based on the size of the object (small units of measurement for small items/large units of measurement for large items). Make a smart guess of how many of the units of measurement fit in the length, width, or height of the item.*

4. Answer: C
Explanation: *Choose which unit of measurement to use based on the size of the object (small units of measurement for small items/large units of measurement for large items). Make a smart guess of how many of the units of measurement fit in the length, width, or height of the item.*

5. Answer: A
Explanation: *Choose which unit of measurement to use based on the size of the object (small units of measurement for small items/large units of measurement for large items). Make a smart guess of how many of the units of measurement fit in the length, width, or height of the item.*

6. Answer: Answers will vary
Explanation: *Choose which unit of measurement to use based on the size of the object (small units of measurement for small items/large units of measurement for large items). Make a smart guess of how many of the units of measurement fit in the length, width, or height of the item.*

7. Answer: Answers will vary
Explanation: *Choose which unit of measurement to use based on the size of the object (small units of measurement for small items/large units of measurement for large items). Make a smart guess of how many of the units of measurement fit in the length, width, or height of the item.*

8. Answer: Answers will vary
Explanation: *Choose which unit of measurement to use based on the size of the object (small units of measurement for small items/large units of measurement for large items). Make a smart guess of how many of the units of measurement fit in the length, width, or height of the item.*

9. Answer: Answers will vary
Explanation: *Choose something that is less than an inch in length. For example a nail.*

10. Answer: Answers will vary
Explanation: *Choose something that is about a centimeters long. For example a small piece of chalk.*

11. Answer: Answers will vary
Explanation: *Choose a smaller unit of measurement (inches or centimeters) for small items. Choose a larger unit of measurement (feet or meters) for large items.*

12. Answer: Answers will vary/ 8 inches
Explanation: *Choose which unit of measurement to use based on the size of the object (small units of measurement for small items/large units of measurement for large items). Make a smart guess of how many of the units of measurement fit in the length, width, or height of the item. Line the object up on the left side of the ruler at 0. See where the end of the object lines up with the ruler. The number it is closest to is how many inches/centimeters in length the object is. Create and solve a subtraction equation to find the difference in the lengths, widths, or heights. Make sure to put the larger number first in the equation.*

13. Answer: Answers will vary/ 5 inches
Explanation: *Choose which unit of measurement to use based on the size of the object (small units of measurement for small items/large units of measurement for large items). Make a smart guess of how many of the units of measurement fit in the length, width, or height of the item. Line the object up on the left side of the ruler at 0. See where the end of the object lines up with the ruler. The number it is closest to is how many inches/centimeters in length the object is. Create and solve a subtraction equation to find the difference in the lengths, widths, or heights. Make sure to put the larger number first in the equation.*

14. Answer: Answers will vary/ 18 centimeters
Explanation: *Choose which unit of measurement to use based on the size of the object (small units of measurement for small items/large units of measurement for large items). Make a smart guess of how many of the units of measurement fit in the length, width, or height of the item. Line the object up on the left side of the ruler at 0 . See where the end of the object lines up with the ruler. The number it is closest to is how many inches/centimeters in length the object is. Create and solve a subtraction equation to find the difference in the lengths, widths, or heights. Make sure to put the larger number first in the equation.*

15. Answer: A

Explanation: *Choose which unit of measurement to use based on the size of the object (small units of measurement for small items/large units of measurement for large items). Make a smart guess of how many of the units of measurement fit in the length, width, or height of the item.*

16. Answer: Mr. James made a better estimation.

Explanation: A fence is closer to 8 feet tall than 15 feet tall.

17. Answer: Answers will vary

Explanation: *Choose a smaller unit of measurement (inches or centimeters) for small items. Choose a larger unit of measurement (feet or meters) for large items.*

18. Answer: Answers will vary

Explanation: *Choose which unit of measurement to use based on the size of the object (small units of measurement for small items/large units of measurement for large items). Make a smart guess of how many of the units of measurement fit in the length, width, or height of the item.*

19. Answer: Answers will vary

Explanation: *Choose a smaller unit of measurement (inches or centimeters) for small items. Choose a larger unit of measurement (feet or meters) for large items.*

20. Answer: Answers will vary

Explanation: *Make a smart guess of how many of the units of measurement fit in the length, width, or height of the item.*

1. Answer: B

Explanation: *Use the draw a picture strategy to solve the addition or subtraction problem.*
34 cm - 12 cm = 22 cm

2. Answer: A

Explanation: *Use the draw a picture strategy to solve the addition or subtraction problem.*
22 inches - 9 inches = 13 inches

3. Answer: B

Explanation: *Use the draw a picture strategy to solve the addition or subtraction problem.*
10 inches + 5 inches = 15 inches

4. Answer: A

Explanation: *Use the draw a picture strategy to solve the addition or subtraction problem.*
25 cm + 8 cm = 33 cm

5. Answer: B

Explanation: *Use the draw a picture strategy to solve the addition or subtraction problem.*
Allen's pen is 10 cm tall. His pencil is 3 cm taller than his pen. 10+3=13. So, Allen's pencil is 13 cm long.

6. Answer: C

Explanation: *Use the draw a picture strategy to solve the addition or subtraction problem.*
Cindy has 3 books stacked on top of each other. Each book is 7 cm tall. 7+7+7=21. So, the 3 books stacked together is 21 cm long.

7. Answer: B

Explanation: *Use the draw a picture strategy to solve the addition or subtraction problem.*
Benny has a drum that is 88 inches tall. His best friend Siena has a drum that is 13 inches shorter than Benny's. 88-13=75
So, Siena's drum is 75 inches tall.

8. Answer:
a. 60 inches
b. 36 inches
Explanation: Lucy has 5 candies that she lines up on the counter. Each candy is 12 inches long. 5 candies together is 12+12+12+12+12=60. Lucy serves 24 inches of the candies to her customers. So, 60-24=36. Lucy is left with 36 inches of candies.

9. Answer: C
Explanation: *Use the draw a picture strategy to solve the addition or subtraction problem.*
Gaynell has a piece of rope that is 42 cm long. He cuts off 8 cm of the rope. 42-8=34. So, Gaynell's rope is 34 cms long.

10. Answer:
a. 69 centimeters
b. 61 centimeters
Explanation: Hanford's table is 58 centimeters long. Amanda's table is 11 centimeters longer than Hanford's table. Amanda's table is 58+11=69 centimeters. Becky's table is 8 centimeters shorter than Amanda's table. So, 69-8=61 Becky's table is 61 cm long.

11. Answer: The foil that is 4 yards long.
Explanation: There are 3 feet in 1 yard. 3+3+3+3=12. There are 12 feet in 4 yards. 12 feet is longer than 7 feet.

12. Answer: B
Explanation: *Use the draw a picture strategy to solve the addition or subtraction problem.*
The train track is 1056 feet long. They add 263 feet to the track. 1056+263=1319. So, the track is 1319 feet long.

13. Answer:The roll of wire that is 2 meters long.
Explanation: There are 100 centimeters in 1 meter. 200 centimeters is longer than 180 centimeters.

14. Answer:
a.32 inches
b. 26 inches
Explanation: Stanley and Joshua make a sandwich that is 24 inches wide. They also make a cheese sandwich that is 8 inches wide.Cheese sandwich is 24+8=32 inches. Their friends eat 6 inches of sandwich So, 32-6=26
They are left with 26 inches of sandwich.

15. Answer: B
Explanation: *Use the draw a picture strategy to solve the addition or subtraction problem.*
A tamarind tree is 33 inches tall. A year later the tree is 89 inches tall. 89-33=56
So, the tamarind tree has grown 56 inches in length.

16. Answer: 47 centimeters
Explanation: *Use the draw a picture strategy to solve the addition or subtraction problem.*
Brian buys a rope that is 55 cm long. He adds another 9 cm to the rope. Then he cuts 17 cm from the rope. 55+9-17=47 So, Brian is left with 47 centimeters.

17. Answer: A
Explanation: *Use the draw a picture strategy to solve the addition or subtraction problem.*
Ronald has a chain that is 230 centimeters long. He also has another chain that is 289 centimeters long. He hooks the chains together. 230+289=519. So, the 2 chains together is 519 cm long.

18. Answer: A
Explanation: *Use the draw a picture strategy to solve the addition or subtraction problem.*
Ryan weighs 83 lbs. Tim weighs 91 lbs. 83+91=174. So, they weigh 174 lbs together.

19. Answer: B
Explanation: *Use the draw a picture strategy to solve the addition or subtraction problem.*
Jason has a bedsheet that is 127 inches wide. Jason has a blanket that is 209 inches wide. 209-127=82. So, Jason is left with 82 inches.

20. Answer: B
Explanation: *Use the draw a picture strategy to solve the addition or subtraction problem.*
The sidewalk in the park is 613 feet long. They add 115 feet to the sidewalk.
613+115=728
So, the sidewalk is 728 feet long.

4.5 GRAPHING AND DATA

1. Answer: 2 symbols for apples and 4 symbols for oranges
Explanation: Each symbol represents 4 fruits. The apple would be represented with 2 symbols. The orange would be represented with 4 symbols.

2. Answer: One clock
Explanation: Use the information from the line plot 3-2 clocks= 1 clock

3. Answer: 12 people
Explanation: According to the data table, there are 4 symbols next to the cheese pizza option. Each symbol represents three people. Therefore, there are 12 people who chose cheese pizza (4x3=12).

4. Answer: A
Explanation: According to the bar graph, there were 9 apple pies and 8 key lime pies at the bake sale. Therefore, there was 1 more apple pie than key lime pie at the bake sale (9-8=1).

5. Answer: B
Explanation: 11 people like red and purple. 9 people like pink and yellow. 11 - 9 = 2.

6. Answer: A
Explanation: According to the bar graph, there were 2 people wearing red shirts and 8 people wearing black shirts. Therefore, there were 6 more people wearing black shirts than red shirts (8-2 = 6).

7. Answer: B
Explanation: Given the table, the crow bird was counted twice as many times as the sparrow.

8. Answer: C
Explanation: According to the bar graph, two toasters are 11 inches tall.

9. Answer: No
Explanation: Answers must include a reasonable explanation such as, "I disagree with Noah because each ice-cream symbol equals 2 people. Therefore, 8 people like chocolate ice-cream and 2 people like vanilla ice-cream. 8 minus 2 is 6. So 6 more people like chocolate than vanilla.

10. Answer: 6
Explanation: The butterfly travels a total of 50 miles over three days. On Monday, the butterfly traveled 12 miles, Tuesday 16 miles. 12 + 16 equals 28. 28 minus 52 equals 24. Each butterfly represents 4 miles so add 6 fours for 24 more miles.

11. Answer: 27
Explanation: Each icon is 3 cakes. Count the icons, multiply the full icons by 3. Add the results: 9, 6, and 12.

12. Answer: D
Explanation: 8 people like broccoli and 5 people like green beans.8 minus 5 is 4 (8-5 = 3).

13. Answer: 35
Explanation: Each icon represents 5 books. The graph contains 7 icons. Multiply 5 by 7 which results in 35 books.

14. Answer: Stamps, Explanation will vary
Explanation: Answers must include a reasonable explanation such as, "Students collected the most stamps because the graph shows 8 stamps collected, whereas students collected less than 8 of each of the other items."

15. Answer: 13
Explanation: The line plot should look like

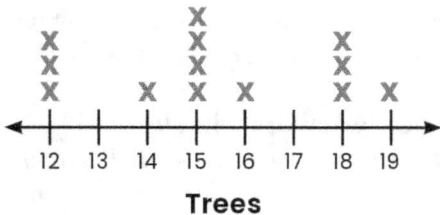

Trees

Add the numbers in the columns for the number of trees. 3 + 1 + 4 + 1 + 3 + 1 = 13.

16. Answer: C
Explanation: The 4 data points for the line plot are 17, 18, 18, and 20. The scale of the line plot should be correctly labeled with the height.

17. Answer: 4, 6, 7, 10
Explanation: Use the rulers to measure the length of each pencil, then record the data in the table.

18. Answer: 5
Explanation: The line plot should show 5 marks at 8 inches, 3 marks at 9 inches, 3 marks at 10 inches, and 2 marks at 11 inches. There are 5 leaves that are 10 inches or longer.

19. Answer: 6
Explanation: The longest cucumber is 22 inches and the shortest cucumber is 16 inches. 22 minus 16 equals 6.

20. Answer: A
Explanation: Use the information from the data table or graph to answer the question. Each icon shows 2 people, so 2 people chose high heels and 6 people chose boots. Therefore, a total of 8 people chose either boots or high heels.

4.6 CHAPTER REVIEW

1. **Answer: A**
Explanation: *It is easiest to measure small objects (less than 1 foot in length) with a ruler.*

2. **Answer: Yardstick.**
Explanation: *It is easiest to measure objects between 1 foot and 1 yard (3 feet) in length with a yardstick.*

3. **Answer: A**
Explanation: A Bamboo tree measures 55 centimeters tall. The next week it measures 75 centimeters tall. The difference is 20 cm. *Use addition or subtraction to solve the word problem. Regroup when needed.*

4. **Answer: They are the same.**
Explanation: 100+100+100+100+100+100=600. There are 100 centimeters in each meter. If you add together the centimeters in 6 meters it equals 600 centimeters.

5. **Answer: B**
Explanation: Rachel is 30 inches tall. Her older brother Bob is 7 inches taller than Rachel. Adding both we get 37 inches which is the height of Gaston. *Use addition or subtraction to solve the word problem. Regroup when needed.*

6. **Answer: A**
Explanation: 12 centimeters is too small for the length of the cucumber. 12 feet and 12 meters are too large for the length of the cucumber.

7.   Answer: A
Explanation: Line the object up on the left side of the ruler at 0. See where the end of the object lines up with the ruler. The number it is closest to is how many inches/centimeters in length the object is.

8.   Answer: 3 inches
Explanation: Inches are longer than centimeters. The number of units is the same, so 3 inches are longer than 3 centimeters.

9.   Answer: Sam is correct
Explanation: 5 inches is too small for the length of a house.

10. Answer: 700 meters
Explanation: Meters are longer than inches.

11.   Answer: C or D
Explanation: *Choose a smaller unit of measurement (inches or centimeters) for small items. Choose a larger unit of measurement (feet or meters) for large items.*

12. Answer: C or D
Explanation: *Choose which unit of measurement to use based on the size of the object (small units of measurement for small items/large units of measurement for large items). Make a smart guess of how many of the units of measurement fit in the length, width, or height of the item.*

13. Answer: Answers will vary
Explanation: *Choose which unit of measurement to use based on the size of the object (small units of measurement for small items/large units of measurement for large items). Make a smart guess of how many of the units of measurement fit in the length, width, or height of the item.*

14. Answer: Answers will vary/18 centimeters
Explanation: *Choose which unit of measurement to use based on the size of the object (small units of measurement for small items/large units of measurement for large items). Make a smart guess of how many of the units of measurement fit in the length, width, or height of the item. Line the object up on the left side of the ruler at 0. See where the end of the object lines up with the ruler. The number it is closest to is how many inches/centimetres in length the object is. Create and solve a subtraction equation to find difference in the lengths, widths, or heights. Make sure to put the larger number first in the equation.*

15. Answer: Answers will vary
Explanation: *Choose a smaller unit of measurement (inches or centimeters) for small items. Choose a larger unit of measurement (feet or meters) for large items.*

16. Answer: A
Explanation: *Use the draw a picture strategy to solve the addition or subtraction problem.*
50cm – 17cm=33cm

17. Answer: B
Explanation: *Use the draw a picture strategy to solve the addition or subtraction problem*
65cm + 12 cm = 77cm

18. Answer: B
Explanation: *Use the draw a picture strategy to solve the addition or subtraction problem*
Cynthia has 4 boxes stacked on top of each other. Each box is 6 cm tall. 6+6+6+6=24
So, the 4 boxes stacked together is 24 cm long.

19. Answer: The foil that is 5 yards long.
Explanation: There are 3 feet in 1 yard. 3+3+3+3+3=15. There are 15 feet in 5 yards. 15 feet is longer than 9 feet.

20. Answer: A
Explanation: Aaron weighs 600 lbs. Timon weighs 727 lbs. 600+727=1327. So, they weigh 1327 lbs. together.

5. TIME AND MONEY

5.1 FOUNDATIONS OF TELLING TIME

1. Answer: A
Explanation: Yes, he is correct.
The minute hand is pointing to the 11, so when you skip count by 5's it means 55 minutes.

2. Answer: B
Explanation: Decide if the event happens in the morning (AM) or afternoon/evening (PM).

3. Answer: A
Explanation: The hour hand (the shorter hand) points to what hour it is. The minute hand (the longer hand) points to what minute it is.

4. Answer: B
Explanation: Decide if the event happens in the morning (AM) or afternoon/evening (PM).

5. Answer: A
Explanation: The correct answer is 8:30 AM
Decide if the event happens in the morning (AM) or afternoon/evening (PM).

6. Answer: B
Explanation: When you are figuring out the hour on an analog clock you will count by 1's. If the hour hand is between two numbers, it means the hour is the first number. Until the hour hand gets all the way to the next number, the hour will still be the first number.

7. Answer: C
Explanation: When figuring out the time on an analog clock you skip count by 1's to figure out the hour and by 5's to figure out the minutes.

8. Answer: D
Explanation: When you are figuring out the hour on an analog clock you will count by 1's. If the hour hand is between two numbers, it means the hour is the first number. Until the hour hand gets all the way to the next number, the hour will still be the first number.

9. Answer: A
Explanation: When you are figuring out the minute on an analog clock you will count by 5's. When the minute hand moves to 0, it means it changes to the next hour and the minutes are 0.

10. Answer: C
Explanation: When you are figuring out the hour on a digital clock you will count by 1's. If the hour hand is between two numbers, it means the hour is the first number. Until the hour hand gets all the way to the next number, the hour will still be the first number.

11. Answer: B
Explanation: Decide if the event happens in the morning (AM) or afternoon/evening (PM).

12. Answer: C
Explanation: When you are figuring out the minute on a digital clock you will count by 5's. When the minute hand moves to 0, it means it changes to the next hour and the minutes are.

13. Answer: A
Explanation: When you are figuring out the minute on an analog clock you will count by 5's. When the minute hand moves to 0, it means it changes to the next hour and the minutes are 0.

14. Answer: D
Explanation: When you are figuring out the hour on a digital clock you will count by 1's. If the hour hand is between two numbers, it means the hour is the first number. Until the hour hand gets all the way to the next number, the hour will still be the first number.

15. Answer: A
Explanation: When you are figuring out the minute on an digital clock you will count by 5's. When the minute hand moves to 0, it means it changes to the next hour and the minutes are 0.

16. Answer: A
Explanation: Decide if the event happens in the morning (AM) or afternoon/evening (PM).

17. Answer: Answers will vary
Explanation: You can tell the time on a clock without numbers in the same way you tell the time on a typical analog clock. Think of where the numbers would be on the clock.

18. Answer: B
Explanation: No, he is incorrect
The hour is listed first on a digital clock, so the hour on the clock is 5.

19. Answer: A
Explanation: Decide if the event happens in the morning (AM) or afternoon/evening (PM).

20. Answer: A
Explanation: When figuring out the time on an analog clock you skip count by 1's to figure out the hour and by 5's to figure out the minutes.

5.2 TELLING TIME TO MINUTES

1. Answer: 4:15, 7:15
Explanation: When you are figuring out the hour on an analog clock you will count by 1's. If the hour hand is between two numbers, it means the hour is the first number. Until the hour hand gets all the way to the next number, the hour will still be the first number. When you are figuring out the minute on an analog clock you will count by 5's. When the minute hand moves to 0, it means it changes to the next hour and the minutes are 0. Figure out what the time would be before or after the time shown on the clock.

2. Answer: An analog clock with the hour hand on 6 and the minute hand on 5
Explanation:

3. Answer: D
Explanation: Hour hand at 4 and minute hand at 12.

4. Answer: B
Explanation: Hour hand at 5 and minute hand at 5.

5. Answer: Hour hand at 6 and minute hand at 6.
Explanation:

6. Answer: Hour hand at 8 and minute hand at 11
Explanation:

7. Answer: Hour hand at 8 and minute hand at 2
Explanation:

8. Answer: Hour hand at 9 and minute hand at 2
Explanation:

9. Answer: B
Explanation: No, she is incorrect.
The hour hand is on the 1 and the minute hand is on the 3. This means the time is 1:15

10. Answer: A
Explanation: Yes, he is correct.
The hour hand is at 4 and the minute hand is at 6. This means the time is 4:30.

11. Answer: C
Explanation: Hour hand at 8 and minute hand at 4. This means the time is 8:20.

12. Answer: A
Explanation: Yes, he is incorrect.
The analog clock shows 5:30 The digital clock shows 5:30.

13. Answer: The hour hand is at 11 and the minute hand is at 2
Explanation:

14. Answer: The hour hand is at 7 and the minute hand is at 9
Explanation:

15. Answer: B
Explanation: Hour hand at 12 and minute hand at 1. This means the time is 12:05.

16. Answer: An analog clock with the hour hand on 8 and the minute hand on 6
Explanation:

17. Answer: 9:30, 8:30
Explanation: When you are figuring out the hour on an analog clock you will count by 1's. If the hour hand is between two numbers, it means the hour is the first number. Until the hour hand gets all the way to the next number, the hour will still be the first number. When you are figuring out the minute on an analog clock you will count by 5's. When the minute hand moves to 0, it means it changes to the next hour and the minutes are 0. Figure out what the time would be before or after the time shown on the clock.

18. **Answer: An analog clock with the hour hand on 9 and the minute hand on 9**
Explanation:

19. **Answer: An analog clock with the hour hand on 6 and the minute hand on 3**
Explanation:

20. **Answer: 5:50**
Explanation: An analog clock with the hour hand on 5 and the minute hand on 10.

> ### 5.3 COUNTING COINS AND BILLS

1. **Answer: A**
Explanation: Briton has $2.00+$2.25 = $4.25. Brady has $4.00. Therefore, Briton has more money than Brady.

2. **Answer: B**
Explanation: No because Sam only has $1.5
0.25+0.25+0.25+0.25+0.25+0.25 = 1.5.

3. **Answer: C**
Explanation: 25+25+25=75¢, Kenny paid 75¢. 75-55 = 20.

4. **Answer: D**
Explanation: 4.00+0.05+0.20=$4.25.

5. **Answer: B**
Explanation: 25+1+1+1+10=38¢.

6. **Answer: A**
Explanation: 1.00+0.25+0.25+0.10=$1.60.
Yes, because she has $1.60.

7. **Answer: B**
Explanation: No because she has 72¢.
25+25+10+10+1+1 = 72¢.

8. **Answer: B**
Explanation: She found $2
1.00+0.25+0.75 = $2.00.

9. **Answer: A**
Explanation: Yes, because she has 40¢.
5+5+5+5+5+5+1+1+1+1+1+1+1+1+1+1 = 40¢.

10. **Answer: D**
Explanation: He spent $2.44
1.00+1.00+0.30+0.04+0.10 = $2.44

11. **Answer: A**
Explanation: Yes, because he has 90¢.
25+25+25+5+5+5 = 90¢.

12. **Answer: A**
Explanation: Quarters are 25. Count the 4 quarters first (25, 50, 75, 100). Dimes are 10. Count the 6 dimes (110, 120, 130, 140, 150, 160). Nickels are 5. Count the 3 nickels (165, 170, 175), Ivy has 125 cents.

13. **Answer: C**
Explanation: She spent $4.20
3.00+0.75+0.15+0.30 = $4.20.

14. **Answer: B**
Explanation: No, because he has $1.60
1.00+0.50+0.10 = $1.60.

15. **Answer: C**
Explanation: 0.05+0.01+0.10=0.16

16. Answer: B
Explanation: 10+10+10+1+1=32¢

17. Answer: A
Explanation: She has $1.55 in her piggy bank
1.00+0.40+0.15=1.55

18. Answer: $2.78
Explanation: 1.00+1.00+0.03+0.50+0.25=$2.78.

19. Answer: A
Explanation: Yes, because two cookies and two chocolates cost 50¢ and he has 72¢.
Total cost of cookies and chocolates=10+10+15+15=50
Victor has 25+25+10+10+1+1=72.

20. Answer: C
Explanation: 4.00+0.25+0.25 = $4.50

5.4 WORD PROBLEMS WITH MONEY

1. Answer: $2.50
Explanation: Saul has $1.25 and Seth has $1.25. Their combined total is $2.50.

2. Answer: B
Explanation: Mia has $3.95. The chicken nuggets and salad will cost $3.65. The other choices cost less or too much.

3. Answer: Noah
Explanation: Liam has $7.00. Noah has $7.50.

4. Answer: D
Explanation: The value of coins and bills she put in the account is $ 5.04. Subtract $ 5.04 from $ 10.90 which equals $ 5.86.

5. Answer: B
Explanation: Briar has 55 cents. Greer has 75 cents. Joe has $1. Altogether they have $2.30.

6. Answer: $0.88
Explanation: 4 quarters, 4 dimes, 6 nickels, and 6 pennies is worth $1.76.
Half of $1.76 is $0.88.

7. Answer: Ava
Explanation: Answers must include a reasonable explanation such as, "Ava has more money because she has $2.75 and Kim has $2.12. $2.75 is greater than $2.12 therefore, Ava has more money than Kim."

8. Answer: Explanations will vary, $0.75 left
Explanation: Answers must include a reasonable explanation such as, "Ryan can exchange his one-dollar bill for 4 quarters. This would allow him to give his friend 1 quarter, or $0.25, and he would have $0.75 the remaining" or any combination of nickels, dimes, and quarters that will allow $0.25 in change.

9. Answer: A
Explanation: She gave 1.00 + 1.00 + 0.20 + 0.20 = $2.40. So, 2.40-1.80=0.6.

10. Answer: B
Explanation: No, because he only has $3.10
1.00+2.00+0.10=3.10.

11. Answer: She can buy one pencil.
Explanation: 1.60+1.60=$3.20.
$3.20 is bigger than $2.65, so she only has money to buy 1 pencil

12. Answer: She can get 12 candies
Explanation: 4 quarters are equal to 1 dollar so she has 12 quarters which equals 3 dollars.

13. Answer: A
Explanation: Yes, because he has $3.10
Tanner has 1.00+8(0.25)+2(0.05)=3.10
3.10 is greater than 3.00.

14. Answer: $0.62 as change
Explanation: Rhett gave 5.00+0.40=$5.40
So, 5.40-4.78=0.62 is his change.

15. Answer: He has $0.02 left.
Explanation: 5.00-4.98=0.02

16. Answer: He will get $0.11 as change
Explanation: 6.00-5.89=0.11

17. Answer: A
Explanation: Rhoda has more money.
Rhoda has 4.00+0.30+0.25=4.55
Ava has 4.00+0.40=4.40
$4.55 is greater than $4.40.

18. Answer: B
Explanation: From the chart, 0.46+0.50=0.96

19. Answer: B
Explanation: Ruby will get $0.05 as change.
Ruby has 2.00+0.40=$2.40
The avocado is $2.35, so 2.40-2.35=$0.05.

20. Answer: A
Explanation: He has the exact amount of money to buy the car. He will not have any money left. Noah has 2+1=3 . The car is $3.00.

5.5 CHAPTER REVIEW

1. Answer: C
Explanation: His sister gives him $0.54, so her brother gives her $1.08.
$2.75 plus $0.54 plus $1.08 equals $4.37.
(2.75+0.54+1.08=4.37)

2. Answer: B
Explanation: The hour hand is past the 12, which means it is right after 12 o'clock. The minute hand points to the 8 and this represents 40 minutes. The time is 12:40.

3. Answer: Agree; Explanation will vary
Explanation: Answers must include a reasonable explanation such as, "I agree with Britta because the little hand is between 11 and 12 which means it is after the 11 o'clock hour. Then 5 added 10 times is 50, so the minutes are 50. Britta is correct it is 11:50."

4. Answer: A
Explanation: Emma will arrive home at 4:00. The hour hand will be on the 4 and the minute hand will be on the 12.

5. Answer: 3:45; Explanations will vary
Explanation: Answers must include a reasonable explanation such as, "Kari's cat finished eating at 3:45 pm. I know because the dog finished eating at 4:00 pm. Adding 45 minutes to 3:15 is 4:00 pm. The cat takes 15 minutes less than the dog to finish its food, which means it finishes eating at 3:45 pm."

6. Answer: D
Explanation: Jenny has $1.10, Vinci has $0.6, Ava has $1.50, Harston has $2.48. The order is Harston, Ava, Jenny, and Vinci.

7. Answer: $8.40
Explanation: Marson puts $2.10 in his bank on Monday. Each following day, he adds $2.10, which means after 4 days, he will have a total of $8.40.

8. Answer: B
Explanation: Music class starts at 3:15. If the class lasts 30 minutes, it ends at 3:45 pm.

9. Answer: The hour hand will be past the 9, and the minute hand will be on the 10.
Explanation: Peter arrived at his grandpa's house at 10:05. He left his house 15 minutes before that, which means he left his house at 9:50.

10. Answer: A
Explanation: 30 minutes before 2:40 is 2:10.

11. Answer: B
Explanation: It takes her 25 minutes to travel home. 25 minutes after 4:45 is 5:10.

12. Answer: 10:00
Explanation: Baking two pans of muffins takes 50 minutes. Fifty minutes past 9:10 am is 10:00 am. The little hand should be on the 10 and the big hand should be on the 12.

13. Answer: 4:05.
Explanation: When drawing the analog clock, the hour hand should be on the 4, and the minute hand should be on the 1. The digital clock should say 4:05.

14. Answer: 5:20
Explanation: 1 hour and 20 minutes have passed.

15. Answer: C
Explanation: The clock shows 3:10. One hour later is 4:10.

16. Answer: 9:30
Explanation: "Half past nine" is 9:30. The small hand on the clock is on the 9 and the large hand is on the 6.

17. Answer: Answers will vary
Explanation: Answers must include a reasonable explanation such as, "35 minutes have passed. I know because I counted by fives starting at the 12 and ending at the 7.

18. Answer: A
Explanation: Zelda has a value of $0.22. Adding $0.44 means there is $0.66.
$(0.22 + 0.44 = 0.66)$

19. Answer: A
Explanation: Yes, she is correct.
They both show the time 1:45.

20. Answer:
Hour hand on 7 and minute hand on 3
Explanation:

6. GEOMETRY

6.1 ATTRIBUTES OF BASIC SHAPES

1. Answer: C
Explanation: A triangle shape is not a quadrilateral.

2. Answer: A
Explanation: Pentagon has 5 sides, so option A is the correct answer.

3. Answer: C
Explanation: A trapezoid is shown in option C, so option C is the correct answer.

4. Answer: 3
Explanation: A triangle has 3 sides.

5. Answer: 6
Explanation: A hexagon has 6 sides.

6. Answer: 4
Explanation: A quadrilateral has 4 corners.

7. Answer: 0
Explanation: A circle has 0 corners.

8. Answer: 2 circles
Explanation:

9. Answer: 1 Hexagon
Explanation:

10. Answer: 4 and 4
Explanation: A rhombus has 4 corners and 4 sides.

11. Answer: False
Explanation: A circle has 0 sides and 0 corners.

12. Answer: Hexagon
Explanation: Sam drew a shape with 6 sides and 6 corners which is a Hexagon.

13. Answer: True
Explanation: The statement is true. A square has 4 sides and 4 corners.

14. Answer: Pentagon
Explanation: The Pentagon has 5 sides and 5 corners.

15. Answer: Robert
Explanation: Robert is correct because a circle must have 0 sides and corners.

16. Answer: Quadrilateral
Explanation: A quadrilateral has 4 sides and 4 corners.

17. Answer: 4
Explanation: The shape of a diamond has 4 sides and 4 corners.

18. Answer: Hexagon
Explanation: A hexagon has 6 sides and 6 corners.

19. Answer: True
Explanation: A rectangle has 4 sides and 4 corners.

20. Answer: Triangle
Explanation: A triangle has 3 sides and 3 corners.

6.2 ATTRIBUTES OF COMPLEX SHAPES

1. Answer: B
Explanation: The answer is option B; because the sides and angles are not equal.

2. Answer: B
Explanation: The answer is option B; because sides and corners are congruent.

3. Answer: 10 sides and 10 corners
Explanation: The shape is a star and has 10 sides and 10 corners.

4. Answer: 16 corners
Explanation: $4+4+4+4=16$
There are 16 corners in total.

5. Answer: 27 corners
Explanation: $5+5+5+6+6=27$
There are 27 corners in total.

6. Answer: Irregular quadrilateral
Explanation: The answer is an irregular quadrilateral.

7. Answer: Irregular pentagon
Explanation: Mike drew an irregular pentagon.

8. Answer: Irregular triangle does not have congruent sides and angles while a regular triangle has congruent sides and angles
Explanation: An irregular triangle does not have congruent sides and angles, while a regular triangle has congruent sides and angles.

9. Answer: True
Explanation: Only the square is regular quadrilateral because all sides and angles are congruent.

10. Answer: Irregular square does not have congruent sides and angles while a regular square has congruent sides and angles
Explanation: An irregular square does not have congruent sides and angles, while a regular square has congruent sides and angles.

11. Answer: 5 sides and 5 corners
Explanation: No matter if it's regular or irregular, a pentagon has 5 sides and 5 corners.

12. Answer: False
Explanation: Irregular polygons have different length of sides and different angles.

13. Answer: Both are correct.
Explanation: Both of them drew the correct irregular triangles because both shapes have different lengths of sides and different angles.

14. Answer: They have 4 sides and 4 corners, a regular square has congruent sides and an irregular square does not have these properties.
Explanation: A regular square and an irregular square are similar because they have 4 sides and 4 corners. They are different because a regular square has congruent sides, and an irregular square does not.

15. Answer: 4 sides and 4 corners
Explanation: It is an irregular quadrilateral because it has 4 sides and 4 corners.

16. Answer: Kindly find below the image.
Explanation:

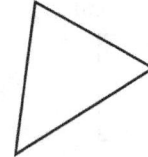

17. Answer: Pentagon
Explanation: It is a regular Pentagon because it has 5 sides and corners

18. Answer: 9 corners
Explanation: 3+3+3=9
There are 9 corners in total.

19. Answer: Becky
Explanation: Becky has a square because a square should have 4 sides and 4 corners.

20. Answer: Regular Hexagon.
Explanation: Jim drew a regular hexagon.

6.3 RECOGNIZE AND DRAW SHAPES

1. Answer: Eli has fewer vertices
Explanation: 6 cubes have 6×8=48 vertices. 4 rectangular prisms have 4×8=32 vertices.

2. Answer: A
Explanation: They both have a triangle shape.

3. Answer: Julian has fewer faces
Explanation: 4 cones have 4×2=8 faces.
4 cylinder have 4×3=12 faces.

4. Answer: A
Explanation: Emma has a square.
A square is a 2D shape that has sides and corners.

5. Answer: D
Explanation: Number of faces in triangular prisms: 5. Number of faces in cubes: 6
Therefore, Total number of faces
of 3 triangular prisms and 3 cubes
=5+5+5+6+6+6=33

6. Answer: A cone has two faces
Explanation: Peyton is wrong because a cone has 2 faces.

7. Answer: A
Explanation: He is correct because a cube has 6 faces.

8. Answer: Cube
Explanation: A cube is a 3-dimensional figure with 6 congruent square faces.

9. Answer: B
Explanation: 3D shape given in the picture is an example of a triangular prism. A triangular prism is a three-dimensional object.

10. Answer: A
Explanation: This is a 2D shape. 2D shapes are flat shapes.

11. Answer: Zero
Explanation: A cylinder is a 3-dimensional figure with a curved rectangular side and a circular top and base. Number of vertices: 0

12. Answer: 12
Explanation: Rectangular prism: A 3-dimensional figure with 6 rectangular faces. Opposite faces are congruent and parallel. It has 12 edges.

13. Answer: B
Explanation:

A sphere is a three-dimensional object that is round in shape. A sphere does not have any faces, edges, or vertices, like other 3D shapes.

14. Answer: D
Explanation: The tomato can is cylinder in shape.

15. Answer: C
Explanation: Number of vertices of the cube: 8. Austin has 4 cubes. Therefore, number of vertices of 4 cubes = 4 × 8 = 32 .

16. Answer: B
Explanation:
Number of faces on a cylinder = 3. Therefore, the number of faces of 3 cylinders 3+3+3 = 9.

17. Answer: A
Explanation: Faces of rectangular prisms = 6 faces of square pyramids = 5
Number of faces in a 2 rectangular prism and 2 square pyramid = 6 + 6 + 5 + 5 = 22.

18. Answer: B
Explanation: Jace has a 3D shape because it has faces, edges, and vertices.

19. Answer: B
Explanation: Square pyramid has a square face on the bottom, and a cube has square faces.They have square faces.

20. Answer: A
Explanation: Parker has more edges. 3 rectangular prisms have 12+12+12= 36 edges and 4 triangular prisms have 9+9+9=27 edges. 36 is greater than 27.

6.4 CHAPTER REVIEW

1. Answer: 3 sides
Explanation: The shape is an irregular triangle and has 3 sides.

2. Answer: 0 vertices
Explanation: The shape is a circle and has 0 vertices.

3. Answer: No
Explanation: A pentagon has 5 vertices. A hexagon has 6 vertices.

4. Answer: Square
Explanation: Square has 4 sides

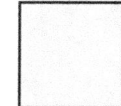

5. Answer: Answers will vary
Explanation: Solutions include a rectangle, a kite, a trapezoid, or any quadrilateral as long as two sides have different lengths.

6. Answer: Option A
Explanation: A quadrilateral has 4 sides and a pentagon has 5 sides.

7. Answer: Circle
Explanation: Circle has 0 sides and 0 corners.

8. Answer: 4 sides
Explanation: A trapezoid has 4 sides.

9. Answer: 8 sides
Explanation: The shape has 8 sides.

10. Answer: Hexagon
Explanation: A hexagon has 6 sides.

11. Answer: True
Explanation: A rhombus has 4 sides.

12. Answer: Triangle
Explanation: Mike drew a triangle, which has 3 sides.

13. Answer: 4 sides
Explanation: A rectangle has 4 sides.

14. Answer: 0 vertices
Explanation: A circle has 0 vertices.

15. Answer: Kindly find the below image
Explanation:

16. Answer: Kindly find the below image
Explanation:

17. Answer: 24 corners
Explanation: 3×4+2×6=12+12=24
There are 24 corners in total.

18. Answer: Irregular pentagon
Explanation: The answer is an irregular pentagon.

19. Answer: True.
Explanation: A regular polygon and an irregular polygon are similar.

20. Answer: 5 sides and 5 corners
Explanation: The shape is an irregular pentagon and has 5 sides and 5 corners.

7. FRACTIONS

7.1 FRACTIONS IN HALVES, THIRDS, AND FOURTHS

1. Answer: B
Explanation: Both parts are the same size and shape.

2. Answer: C
Explanation: The given shape is divided into two equal parts. 1 out of 2 parts is shaded. Therefore, the fraction is $\frac{1}{2}$.

3. Answer: A
Explanation: The 3 parts are the same size.

4. Answer: Thirds
Explanation: The orange is divided into 3 parts.

5. Answer: D
Explanation: The 4 parts are the same size.

6. Answer: C
Explanation: The given triangle has 4 parts. 1 out of 4 parts is shaded.

7. Answer: B
Explanation: In the given rectangle, 1 out of 4 parts is shaded.

8. Answer: Fourths
Explanation: The given shape is divided into fourths.

9. Answer: 8
Explanation: The given shape has 8 equal parts.

10. Answer: Yes
Explanation:
They both represent three-fourths.

11. Answer: No
Explanation: The first shape represents three-fourths and the second shape represent two-fourths.

12. Answer: Two-fourths
Explanation: They both represent two-fourths.

13. Answer: Three-fourths
Explanation: Only one part is missing, and the other three parts are remaining.

14. Answer: One-third
Explanation: Only one tomato is circled.

15. Answer: Two-thirds
Explanation: Two tomatoes out of three are not circled.

16. Answer: Three-fourths
Explanation: There are four equal parts. Matthew has three-fourths of the pie remaining.

17. Answer: One-fourth
Explanation: There are four equal parts in a cake. Maria gave two parts to her mom and one part to her dad. She gave a total of 3 parts. So she has one part left.

18. Answer:

Explanation: The given trapezoid is partitioned into halves.

19. Answer:

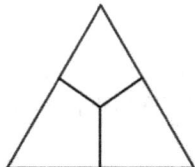

Explanation: The given triangle is partitioned into thirds.

20. Answer: Four
Explanation: The given circle has 4 equal parts.

7.2 PARTITIONING CIRCLES AND RECTANGLES

1. Answer: B
Explanation: The circle is divided into three equal parts.

2. Answer: C
Explanation: A rectangle is divided into two equal parts. One part is shaded.

3. Answer:

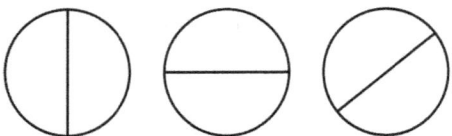

Explanation: Three circles are divided into halves in three different ways.

4. Answer:

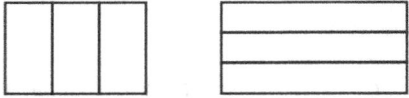

Explanation: Two rectangles are divided into thirds in two different ways.

5. Answer:

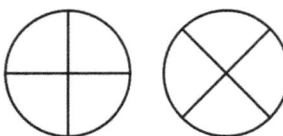

Explanation: Two circles are divided into fourths in two different ways.

6. Answer: B
Explanation: There are four parts of an apple. Jack and Ian together got 2 parts.

7. Answer: C
Explanation: The cupcake is divided into four equal parts. Sam ate one part and there are three parts remaining.

8.   Answer: B
Explanation: The circle B is divided into two equal parts.

9.   Answer: $\frac{1}{2}$

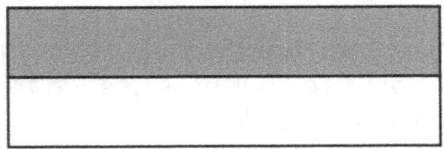

Explanation: The first rectangle is divided into two equal shares. So the fraction is $\frac{1}{2}$.

10. Answer: B
Explanation: As option B shows, the pizza is cut into three equal pieces.

11. Answer: A
Explanation: The rectangle is colored two-fourths in option A.

12. Answer: B
Explanation: The circle is divided into four equal parts, but not shaded into two-fourths. Four parts are shaded.

13. Answer: A
Explanation: The given rectangle is divided into four equal parts and three-fourths are shaded.

14. Answer:

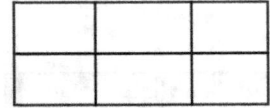

Explanation: The given rectangle is divided into six equal parts.

15. Answer: A
Explanation: The circle is divided into two equal parts, and one half is shaded.

16. Answer: C
Explanation: The rectangle is divided into seven parts.

17. Answer: C
Explanation: The rectangle has five shaded parts.

18. Answer: B
Explanation: Circle B has three shaded parts.

19. Answer: D
Explanation: Circle D has eight parts.

20. Answer:

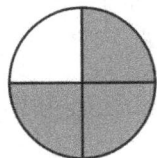

Explanation: The circle has four parts. Three-fourths of the circle are shaded.

<hr/>

7.3 WHOLES

1. Answer: A
Explanation: Franklin has 7 toy cars. So $\frac{7}{1}$ is the correct option.

2. Answer: D
Explanation: Ronald cut a watermelon into 12 pieces. The total number of pieces of a watermelon is 12. So the fraction is $\frac{12}{12}$.

3. Answer:

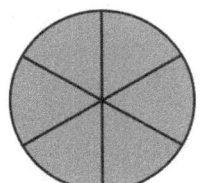

Explanation: The lines are drawn to show $\frac{6}{6}$.

4. Answer: B
Explanation: The numerator and denominator have the same value 5. So the value is 1.

5. Answer: C
Explanation: The value is 9.

6. Answer: C
Explanation: The number line C shows the fraction $\frac{8}{1}$.

7. Answer: B
Explanation: The option B shows three equal parts and three parts are shaded.

8. Answer: A

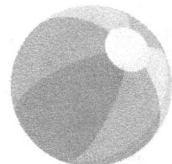

Explanation: The first picture shows the fraction $\frac{1}{1}$.

9. Answer: A
Explanation:

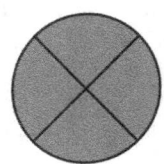

10. Answer: B
Explanation: Option B shows the whole.

11. Answer: B
Explanation:

12. Answer: C
Explanation: In option C, two circles are not shaded.

13. Answer: A
Explanation: Three parrots are in the cage.

14. Answer: Correct
Explanation: He is correct because there are a total of 8 pieces and all the pieces were eaten.

15. Answer: $\frac{2}{2}$
Explanation: There are 2 pieces of dragon fruit and he gave two pieces to his brother and sister. So the fraction is $\frac{2}{2}$.

16. Answer: B
Explanation: $\frac{3}{1}$ = 3 wholes

17. Answer: B
Explanation: In option B, the circle is divided into 10 shares and shaded $\frac{10}{10}$.

18. Answer: Two-fourths
Explanation: Two-fourths is needed to make the whole circle shaded.

19. Answer: A
Explanation: $\frac{2}{4} + \frac{2}{4} = \frac{4}{4} = 1$

20. Answer: A
Explanation: $\frac{2}{2}$ = 1

7.4 CHAPTER REVIEW

1. Answer: D
Explanation: The cake is divided into three equal shares.

2. Answer:

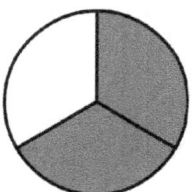

Explanation: The circle should be divided into three equal parts, of which two are shaded.

3. Answer:

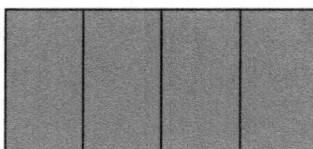

Explanation: The rectangle should be partitioned into four equal parts, with all parts shaded.

4. Answer: One-fourth
Explanation: Solution includes $\frac{1}{4}$.

5. Answer: 1
Explanation: The fraction means 5 of 5 equal parts. So one whole.

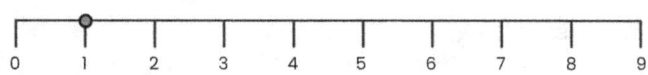

6. Answer: $\frac{3}{4}$
Explanation: The circle is divided into 4 parts. Three parts are shaded.

7. Answer: $\frac{1}{4}$
Explanation: The rectangle is divided into 4 parts. One part is shaded.

8. Answer: One-third
Explanation: The rectangle is divided into 3 parts. One part is shaded.

9. Answer: Halves
Explanation: The given shape is divided into halves.

10. Answer: Yes
Explanation: Both shapes represent the same fraction of five parts shaded out of six.

11. Answer: One-fourth
Explanation: There are three rats and one dog.

12. Answer:

Explanation: The given heart shape is divided into halves.

13. Answer: True
Explanation: The rhombus is divided into four equal parts, and four of those parts are shaded.

14. Answer:

Explanation: The circle is divided into 12 equal parts.

15. Answer: B
Explanation: The whole rectangle is shaded.

16. Answer: D
Explanation: Donald has 5 notebooks. So $\frac{5}{1}$ is the correct option.

17. Answer: A
Explanation: Bristol cut a cucumber into 15 pieces. The total number of pieces in a cucumber is 15. So the fraction is $\frac{15}{15}$.

18. Answer: C
Explanation: The number line C shows the fraction $\frac{9}{9} = 1$.

19. Answer: B
Explanation: In option B, $\frac{4}{1}$ rectangles are not shaded.

20. Answer: D
Explanation: $\frac{1}{3} + \frac{2}{3} = \frac{3}{3} = 1$

COMPREHENSIVE ASSESSMENT

ASSESSMENT – 1

1. Answer: 26
Explanation: 43 plus 31 equals 74. The farmer has picked 74 vegetables. 100 –74 = 26.

2. Answer: 5
Explanation: There are 5 rows, so he should add the number 3 five times.

3. Answer: 653; Explanation will vary
Explanation: Answers must include a reasonable explanation such as,
" 600 + 50 + 3 is the expanded form of 653. I know because 600 is 6 hundreds, 50 is 5 tens and 3 is three ones. 6 hundreds, 5 tens and 3 ones is 653."

4. Answer: Disagree; Explanation will vary
Explanation: Answers must include a reasonable explanation such as, "I disagree. To compare these numbers, you should look at the hundreds place; 8 hundreds are more than 6 hundreds, so you don't need to look at the tens."

5. Answer: A
Explanation: 15 yards is the best estimate. The other choices are too short or too long.

6.Answer: B
Explanation: Andy's sailboat is 20 feet long.

7. Answer: B
Explanation: There are 3 hundreds in 375.

8. Answer: A
Explanation: When counting by 5's, 560 comes after 555.

9. Answer: A
Explanation: 60 + 55 + 80 =195 kilograms.

10. Answer: 133 flowers
Explanation: 50 plus 8 plus 75 (5) equals 133.

11. Answer: A
Explanation: Sam has 150+ 110 = 260 marbles.

12. Answer: 800+50+3
Explanation: 800+50+3 is the expanded form of 853.

13. Answer: 690
Explanation: Strategies should involve or describe regrouping for addition. Standard algorithm to add ones (0 +0 =0), tens (70+ 20 = 90, or regrouping to show there are 0 tens), and hundreds (500 + 100 =600). The sum is 690.

14. Answer: No; Explanation will vary
Explanation: Answers must include a reasonable explanation such as, "Victoria is incorrect because instead of rounding 77 to 80, she should have rounded down to 70. She subtracted the ones (7-4) separately, which left subtraction of the tens (70-20). No regrouping is required for this expression, so the correct decomposition strategy would be (70-20)+(7-4). The correct answer is 53."

15. Answer: A
Explanation: 858 is one number directly before 859.

16. Answer: A
Explanation: 170+7 = 177 cm.

17. Answer: A
Explanation: To find the total number of points add 62+21=83.

18. Answer: C
Explanation: This is a two-step problem. Step 1: Subtract 4 from 18. Step 2: Add 5 to the answer. (18 -4) + 5 = 19.

19. Answer: Option A.
Explanation: Sam's farm is 1826 meters wide. Mike's farm is 2265 centimeters wide. Adding both we get 4091 meters which is the length of farms put together.
Use addition or subtraction to solve the word problem. Regroup when needed.

20. Answer: B
Explanation: 5+5+5+5+5+5+5+5+5+5=50
Allen partitioned a rectangle into 5 columns and 10 columns, so it makes 50 units.

21. Answer: B
Explanation: The number Jim picked is 2571, which is an odd number. It ends with 1, so it is an odd number. Any number that ends with 1,3,5,7,9 is an odd number.

22. Answer: A
Explanation: 4 more than 220 is 224
224 is an even number because it ends with 4.Any number that ends with 2,4,6,8,0 is an even number.

23. Answer: A
Explanation: the total sum of 1090 and 1102 is 2192. 2192 is an even number because it ends with 2. Any number that ends with 2,4,6,8,0 is an even number.

24. Answer: C
Explanation: Subtract one to the number in the tens place. The rest of the number stays the same. Andes has 52 books 15 is given, so (52-15=37) books.

25. Answer: A
Explanation: 6322 is the larger number
Decide if the first number is larger, the second number is larger, or the numbers are the same.

26. Answer: A
Explanation: Subtract one from the number in the hundreds place. The rest of the number stays the same.

27. Answer: Thousands - 2, Hundreds - 5, Tens -6, Ones - 4
Explanation: In the number 2564 there is 4 in the one's place, 6 in the tens place, 5 in the hundreds place, 2 in the thousands place.

28. Answer: A
Explanation: Decide if the event happens in the morning (AM) or afternoon/evening (PM).

29. Answer: B
Explanation: No because Sushi only has $1.5, and the juice costs $3.35
0.25+0.25+0.25+0.25+0.25+0.25 = 1.5.

30. Answer: Three-fourths
Explanation: There are four-equal parts. Maria has three fourths of pie.

31. Answer: A
Explanation: Four parrots are in the cage.

32. Answer: B
Explanation: The cupcake is divided into three equal parts. Sam ate one part and the remaining part is two.

33. Answer: The given shape is a cylinder.
Explanation: Given that, the shape has 2 faces, 0 vertices, and 0 edges. Therefore, the shape is a cylinder.

34. Answer: 4
Explanation: A rectangle has 4 vertices.

35. Answer: A
Explanation: It is known that a Pentagon is a 2D shape with 5 sides and 5 vertices.

36. Answer: A
Explanation: A semicircle is made of a straight line and a curve. It has 2 corners where the ends of the straight line meet with the curved shape.

37. Answer: B
Explanation: Vertically line up the numbers you are adding, so that each place value is in the same vertical line. Start adding with the one's place value and move to the large place values. In a marriage hall, there were 300 Men, 150 Women, 100 Elderly people, and 110 kids. (300+150+100+110=660)
So, there were 660 guests altogether.

38. Answer: A
Explanation: Start by adding in the ones place value and then move to the larger place values. Regroup one's into tens and tens into ones when needed when there is a group of 10 or more ones or tens. A group of people, 105 order noodles and 123 order pasta.

39. Answer: A
Explanation:
Use the counting up strategy to solve the problem.
Aaron is 10 years old and Kim is double the age of Aaron, so 10+10=20.
Kim's age is 20 years.

40. Answer: 6951
Explanation: *Start by adding in the one's place value and then move to the larger place values. Regroup ones into tens and tens into ones when needed when there is a group of 10 or more ones or tens.*
5895+1056=6951

41.Answer: A
Explanation: *Start by adding in the one's place value and then move to the larger place values. Regroup ones into tens and tens into ones when needed when there is a group of 10 or more ones or tens.*
355+255=610

42. Answer: B
Explanation:
Start by subtraction in the one's place value. Then, move to the larger place values. Regroup tens into ones and hundreds into tens when needed.
Tom bought two gold chains for 5120 dollars. The first chain is 3336 dollars.
(5120-3336=1784)The price of the second chain is 1784 dollars.

43. Answer: A
Explanation:
Start by subtracting in the one's place value. Then, move to the larger place values. Regroup tens into ones and hundreds into tens when needed.
In a box of Fig, there are 650 figs. 315 fig are labeled, remaining are unlabeled.
(650-315=335)So, there are 335 figs unlabeled.

44. Answer: A
Explanation: There were 120 parrots in a cage. Stella bought and let 15 parrots free. (120 - 15 = 105) So, there were 105 parrots still in the cage.

45. Answer: A
Explanation:
Start by subtracting the one's place value. Then, move to the larger place values. Regroup tens into ones and hundreds into tens when needed
There are 100 students in a class. Out of that 17 are from Hostel.(100-17=83) So, 83 students come from home.

COMPREHENSIVE ASSESSMENT

ASSESSMENT - 2

1.Answer: 534, Explanation will vary
Explanation: Answers must include a reasonable explanation such as, "You are thinking of 534. I know because 534 have 5 hundreds, 3 tens, and 4 ones, or 500+3+4."

2. Answer: 432, Explanation will vary
Explanation: Answers must include a reasonable explanation such as, "Celsia has 417 apples. If we add 15 to 417, the answer is 432."

3. Answer: A
Explanation: 8+7=15

4. Answer: $90
Explanation: $330 - $120 - $120 = $90

5.Answer: B
Explanation: 50 + 15 = 65cm

6. Answer: A
Explanation: A triangle is a two- dimensional shape. The other shapes are three-dimensional shapes.

7. Answer: Seven hundred and twenty-three
Explanation: Seven hundred and twenty-three is the word form of 723.

8. Answer: 581 > 322
Explanation: Five hundred eighty-one is greater than three hundred twenty-two can be written as 581 > 322. The symbol always points to the smaller side.

9. Answer: 9
Explanation: 3 groups of 3 is 9.

10. Answer: 460
Explanation: 460 is 4 hundreds and 6 tens, 400 + 60.

11. Answer: B
Explanation: 570 is greater than 507.

12. Answer: B
Explanation: 21-17=4

13. Answer: A
Explanation: 34 centimeters is a good estimate.

14. Answer: 70
Explanation: Jim scores 43 points, John scores 55 points (43 + 12), and Jill scores 70 points (55 +15).

15. Answer: A
Explanation: Steve's cone is 10 inches tall, Tom's ice cream cone is 7 inches tall, and Allen's cone is 9 inches tall.

16. Answer: 200 grams
Explanation: 1100 −600 - 300 = 200 grams

17. Answers: A
Explanation: *Use the draw-a-picture strategy to solve the addition or subtraction problem*
20 inches + 15 inches = 35 inches

18. Answers: Answers will vary
Explanation: Choose something that is about a centimeter long. For example, a small piece of chalk.

19. Answers: Choice A is the correct answer
Explanation: Choose which unit of measurement to use based on the size of the object (small units of measurement for small items/large units of measurement for large items). Make a smart guess of how many of the units of measurement fit in the length, width, or height of the item.

20. Answers: 25 feet
Explanation: Yards are longer than feet. The number of units is the same, so 25 feet is shorter than 25 yards.

21. Answers: C
Explanation: The answer is option C, 18 units. So, after adding 3 columns, Eda has a rectangle with 18 units.

22. Answers: 6 books.
Explanation: Robert has 6 books. 3+3=6

23. Answers: B
Explanation: There is a 3 in the hundreds place, which has a value of 300. There is a 3 in the tens place, which has a value of 30. There is a 5 in the ones place, which has a value of 5.

24. Answers: A
Explanation: 6352 is the larger number Decide if the first number is larger, the second number is larger, or the numbers are the same.

25. Answers: A
Explanation: 1155
Subtract one from the number in the tens place. The rest of the number stays the same.

26. Answers: C
Explanation: Answers will vary
There is a 3 in the hundreds place, which has a value of 300. This can be expressed as three hundred. That is the word that is missing.

27. Answer: B
Explanation: Zenas has a value of $0.44. Adding $0.50 means there is $0.94. (0.44+0.50=0.94)

28. Answer: C
Explanation: The clock shows 3:10.

29. Answer: She will get $0.5 as a change
Explanation: 5.00 - 4.5 = 0.5.

30. Answer: A
Explanation: Two cookies and two chocolates cost 70¢ and Vensia has 72¢.
Total cost of cookies and chocolates = 15+15+20+20 = 70
Vensia has 25+25+10+10+1+1 = 72.

31. Answer: D
Explanation: The cake is divided into three equal shares. So the share is thirds.

32. Answer: B
Explanation: $\frac{3}{1}$ = 3 wholes

33. Answer: D
Explanation: Ronald cut thewatermelon into 10 pieces. The total number of pieces of a watermelon is 10. So the fraction is $\frac{10}{10}$.

34. Answer:

Explanation: The above figure shows a closed shape with three sides.

35. Answer: The shape is a cylinder.
Explanation: A shape with curved surfaces and circular faces at the top and bottom is a cylinder.

36. Answer: A diamond shape will be formed.
Explanation: If a triangle and an inverted triangle are combined, a diamond shape will be formed.

37. Answer:

Explanation: It is known that a diamond is a 2D shape with 4 vertices and 4 sides. Therefore, the required figure is as obtained above.

38.Answer:

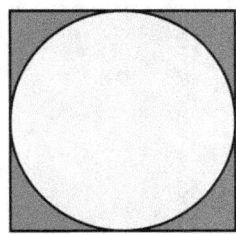

Explanation: Given that, the shape of the gift is formed by using a shape with four sides and four corners and then inscribing a shape inside it with no edges or vertices. Thus, the required shape is as shown above.

39. Answer: A cuboid has 12 edges.
Explanation: It is known that a cuboid is a 3D image with 8 vertices, 6 faces and 12 edges. Therefore, a cuboid will have 12 edges.

40. Answer: The shape is a circle.
Explanation:

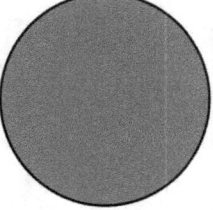

A shape with 0 vertices and 0 sides is a circle.

41. Answer: D
Explanation: Use the counting-up strategy to solve the problem. Shirley has 55 figs, then she gets 20 more figs, so 55+20=75. Now Shirley has 75 Figs.

42. Answer: C
Explanation: *Try to answer the question from memory or in your head. If you need help, use the counting up (addition) or counting down (subtraction) strategies to solve the problem.*
(46+56=102) So, Robert has 102 ribbons in total.

43. Answer: B
Explanation: *Start by subtraction in the one's place value. Then, move to the larger place values. Regroup tens into ones and hundreds into tens when needed.*
Helen has taken 50 books from the library. He just finished reading 15 books. (50 - 15 = 35) So, 35 books need to be completed by Helen.

44. Answer: C
Explanation: *Start by subtracting in the one's place value. Then, move to the larger place values. Regroup tens into ones and hundreds into tens when needed.*
In a 650 group of people,500 people loved coffee, and the other group loved tea. (650-500=150) So, 150 people loved tea.

45. Answer: C
Start by subtracting the ones place value. Then, move to the larger place values. Regroup tens into ones and hundreds into tens when needed
Sherin has 455 bottles. Linda has 155 bottles. (455-155=300) So, Sherin has 300 bottles more than Linda.